I0442931

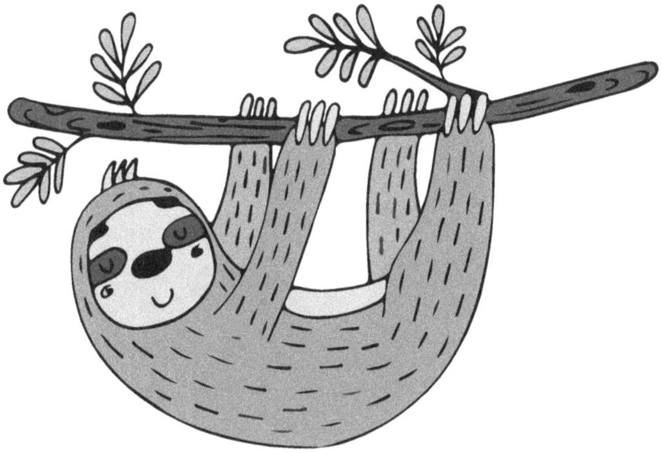

THIS BOOK BELONGS TO :

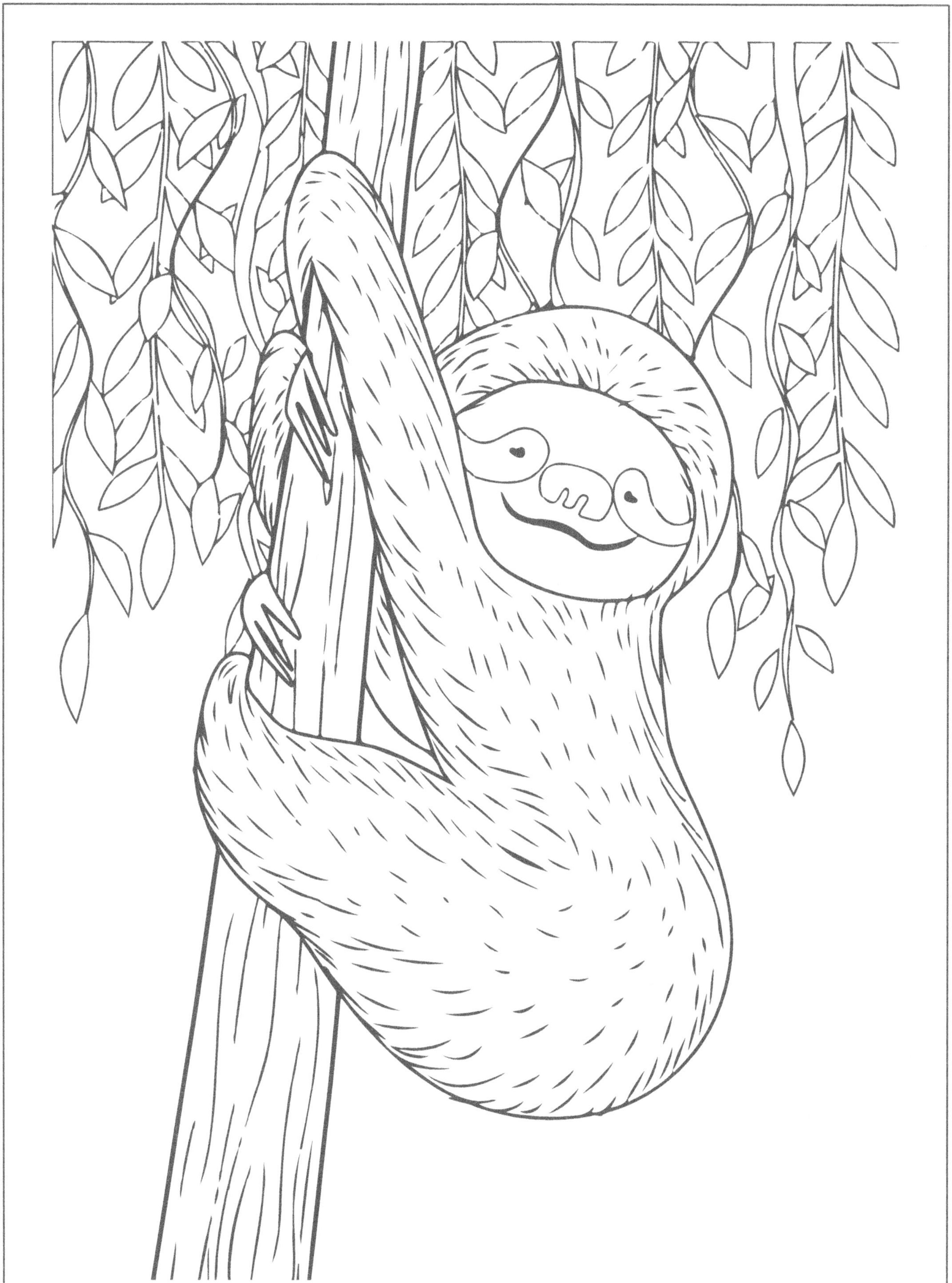

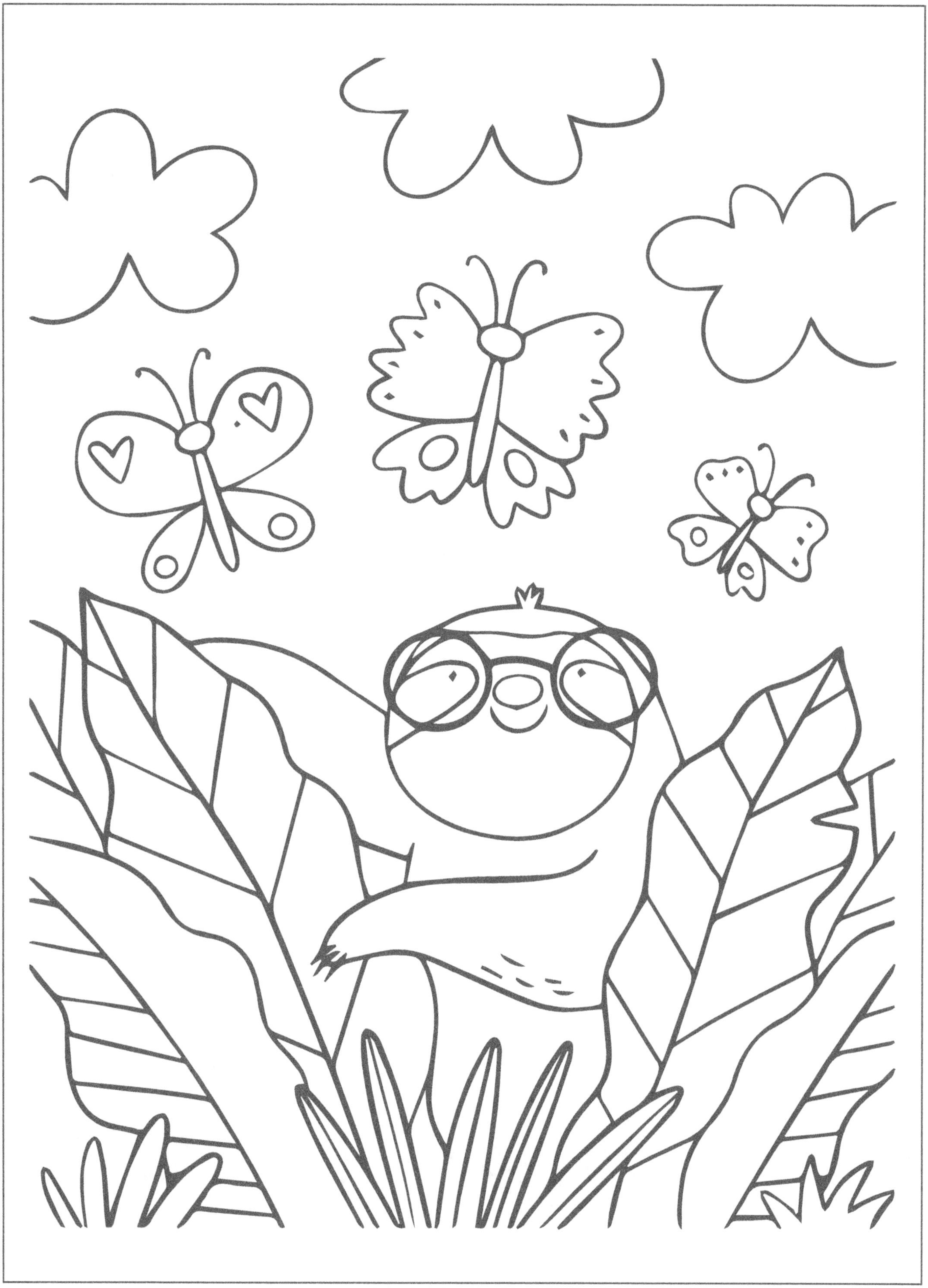

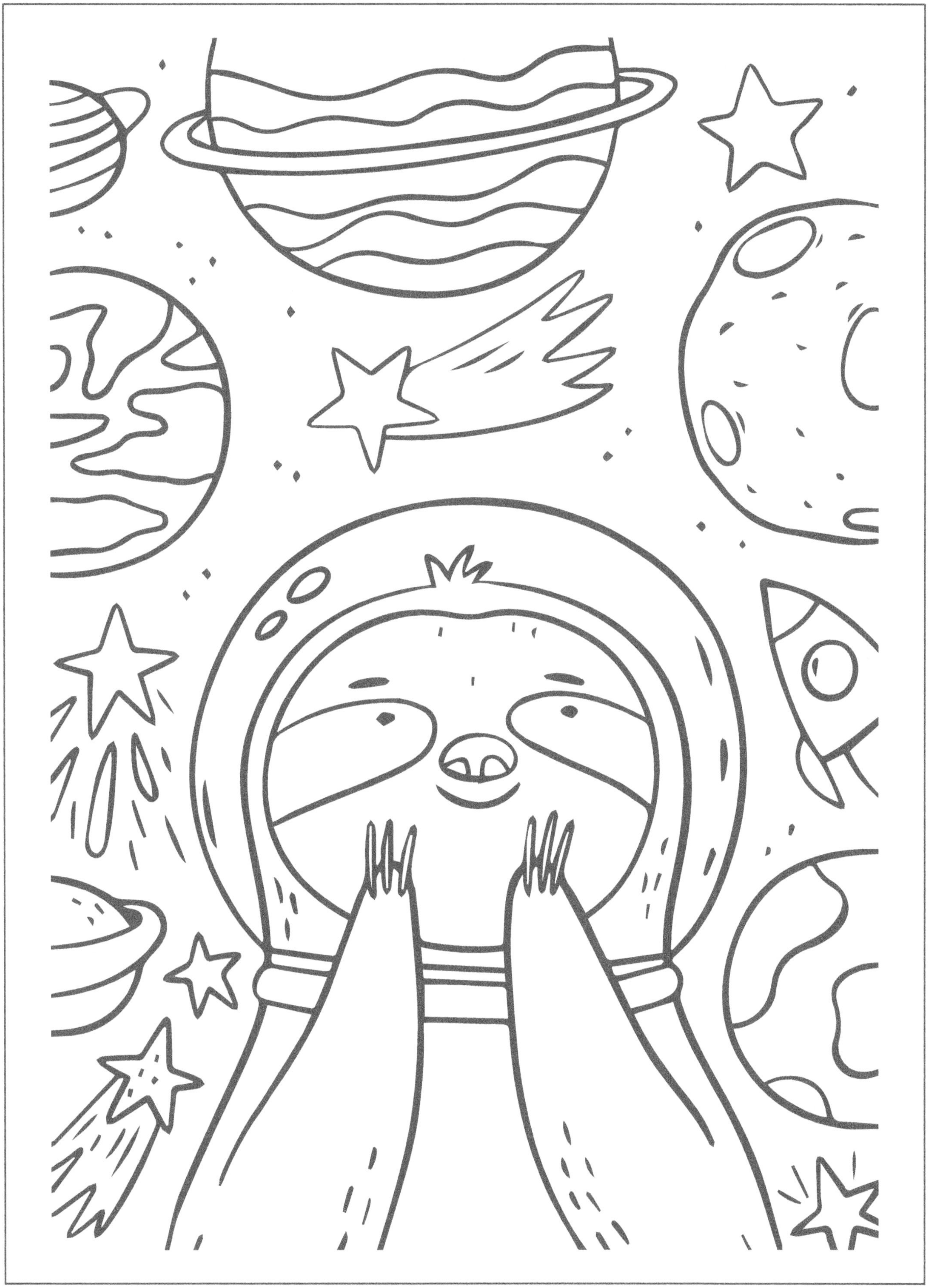

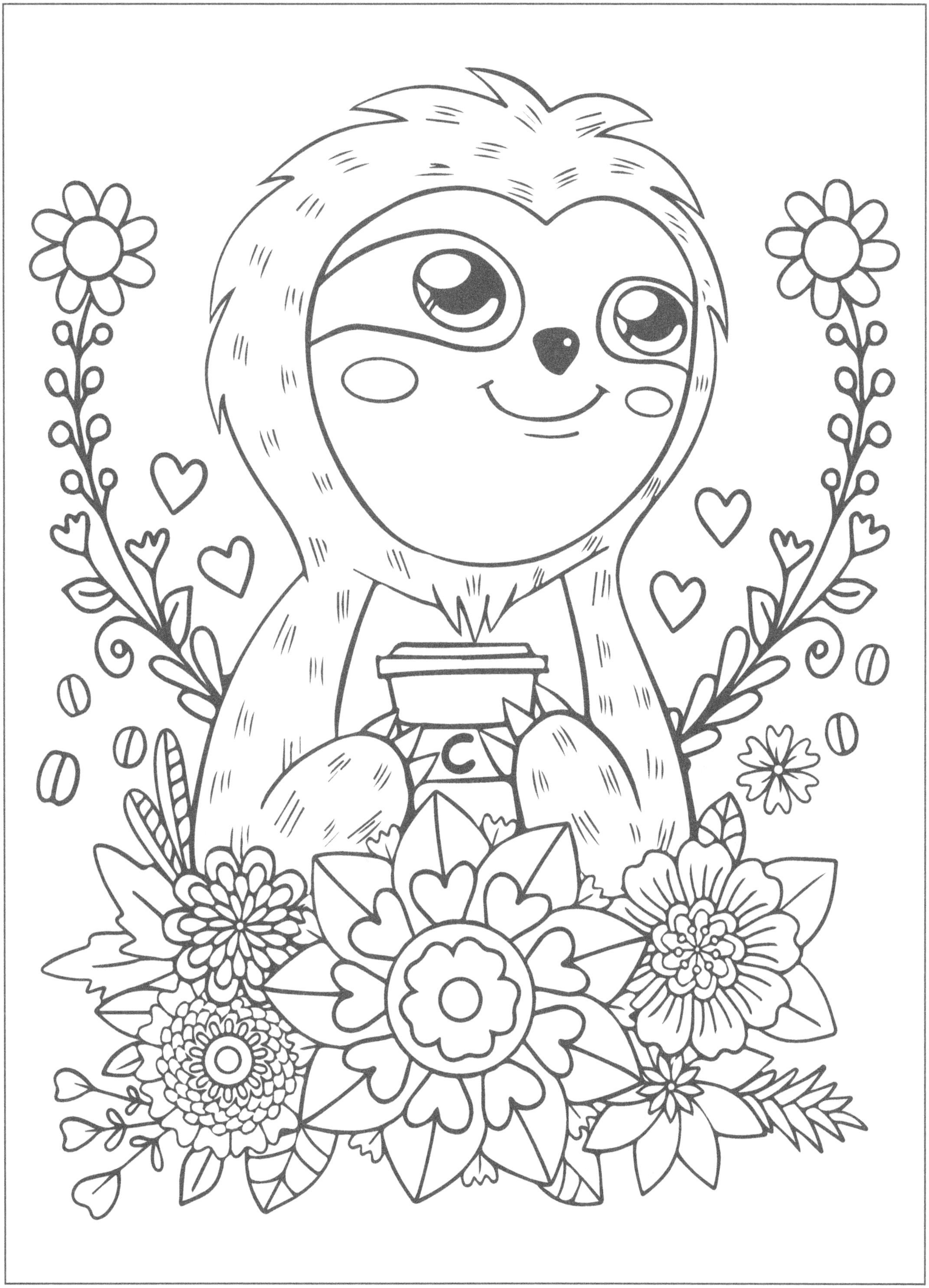
C

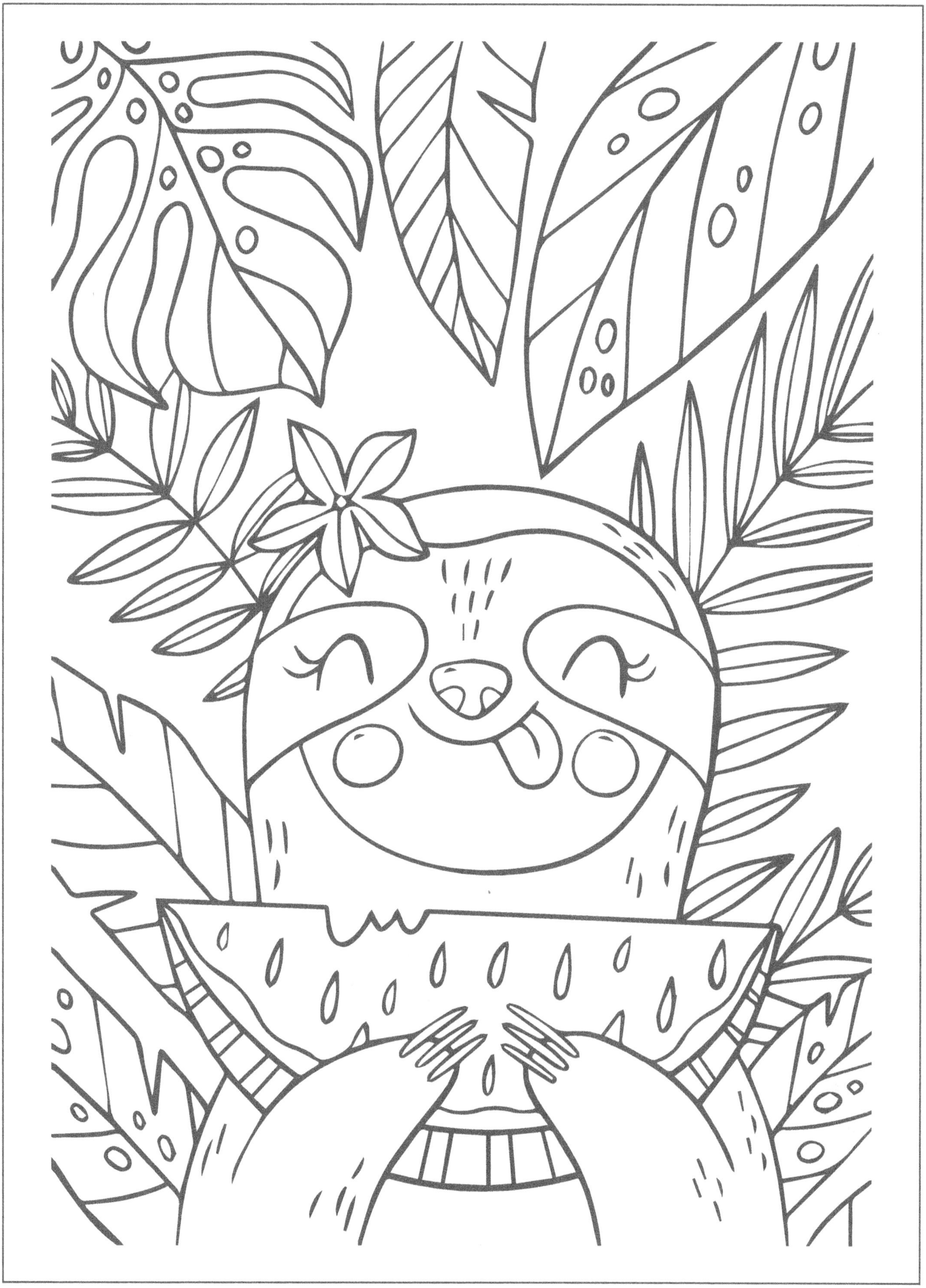

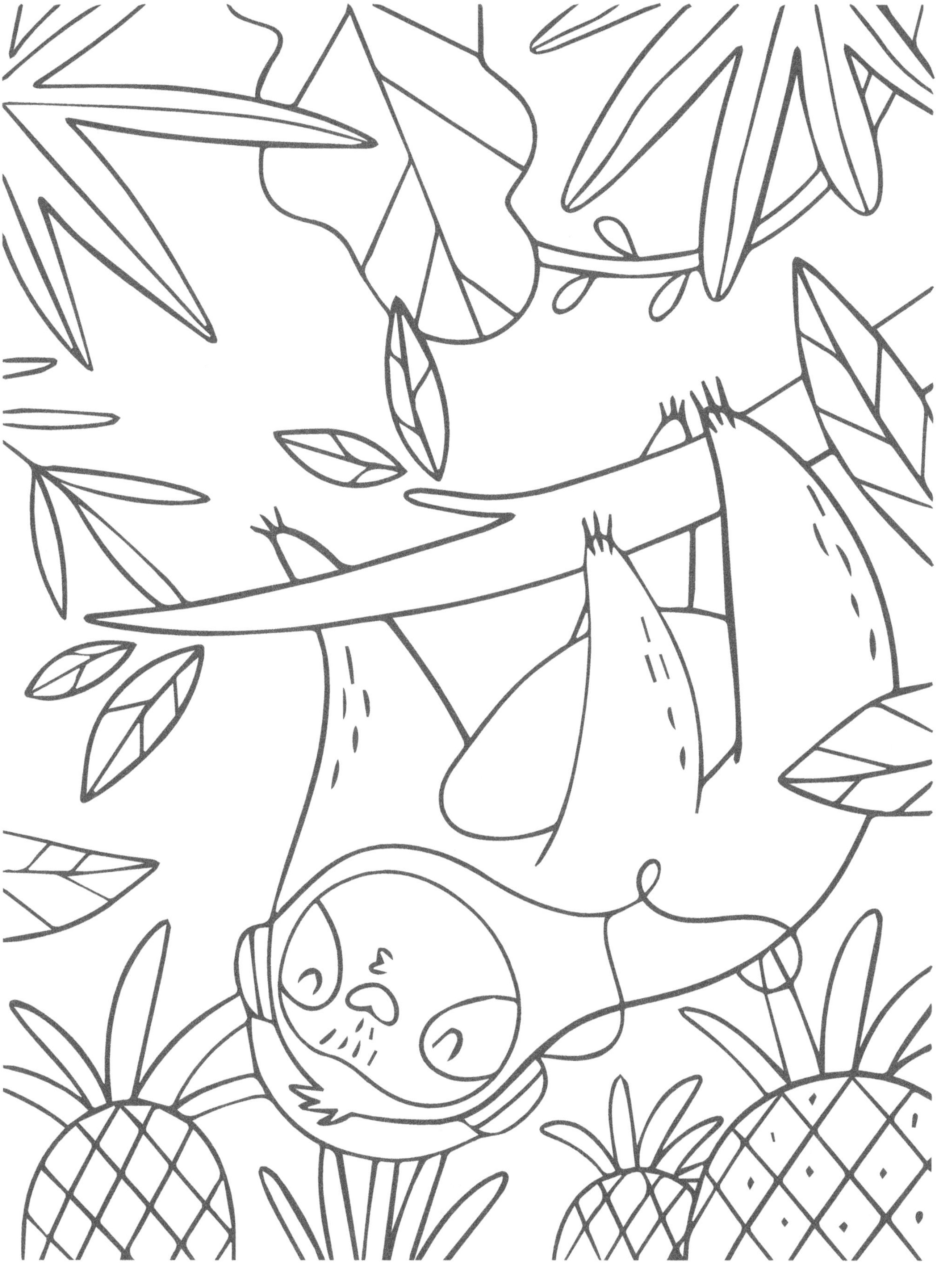

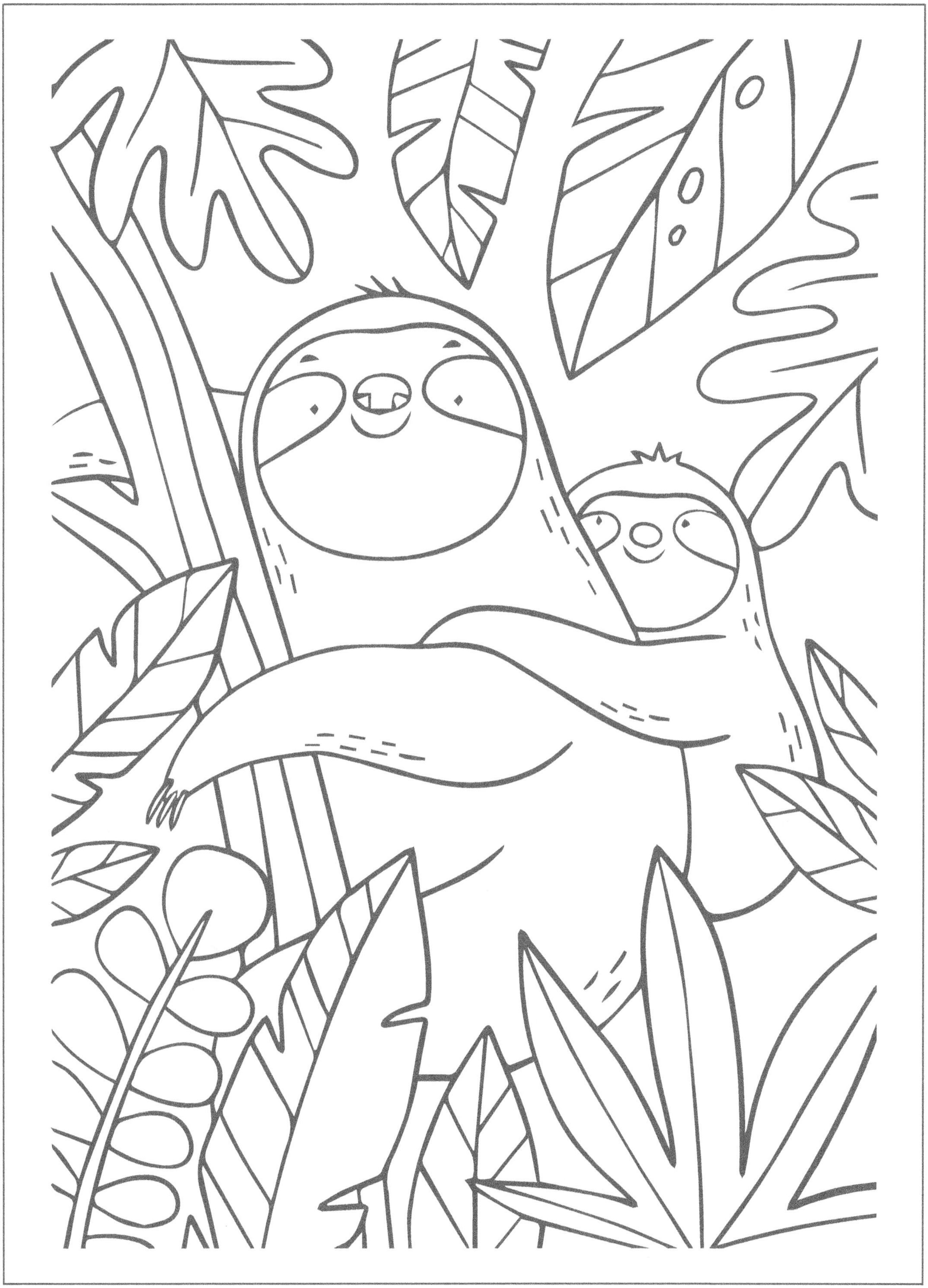

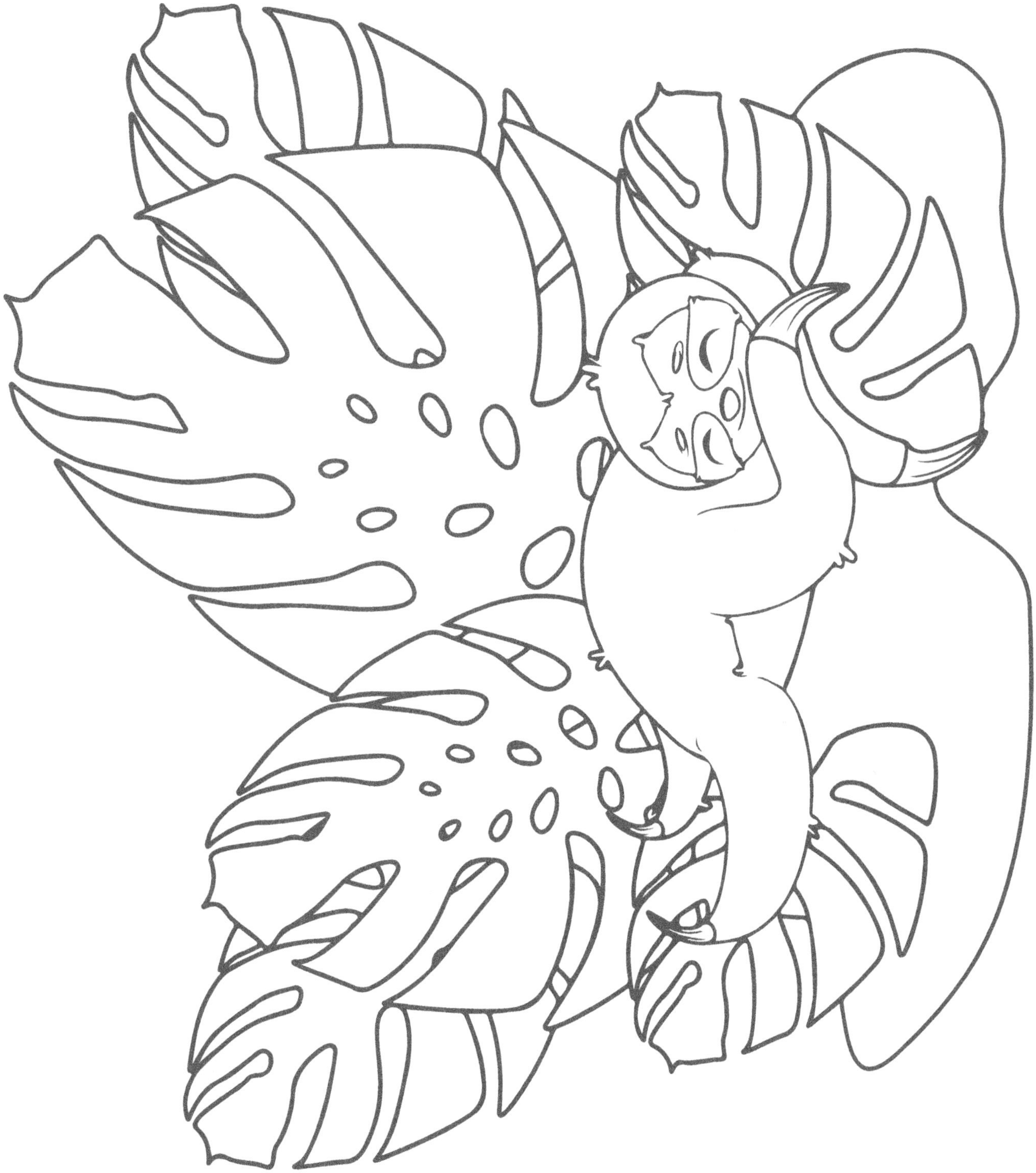

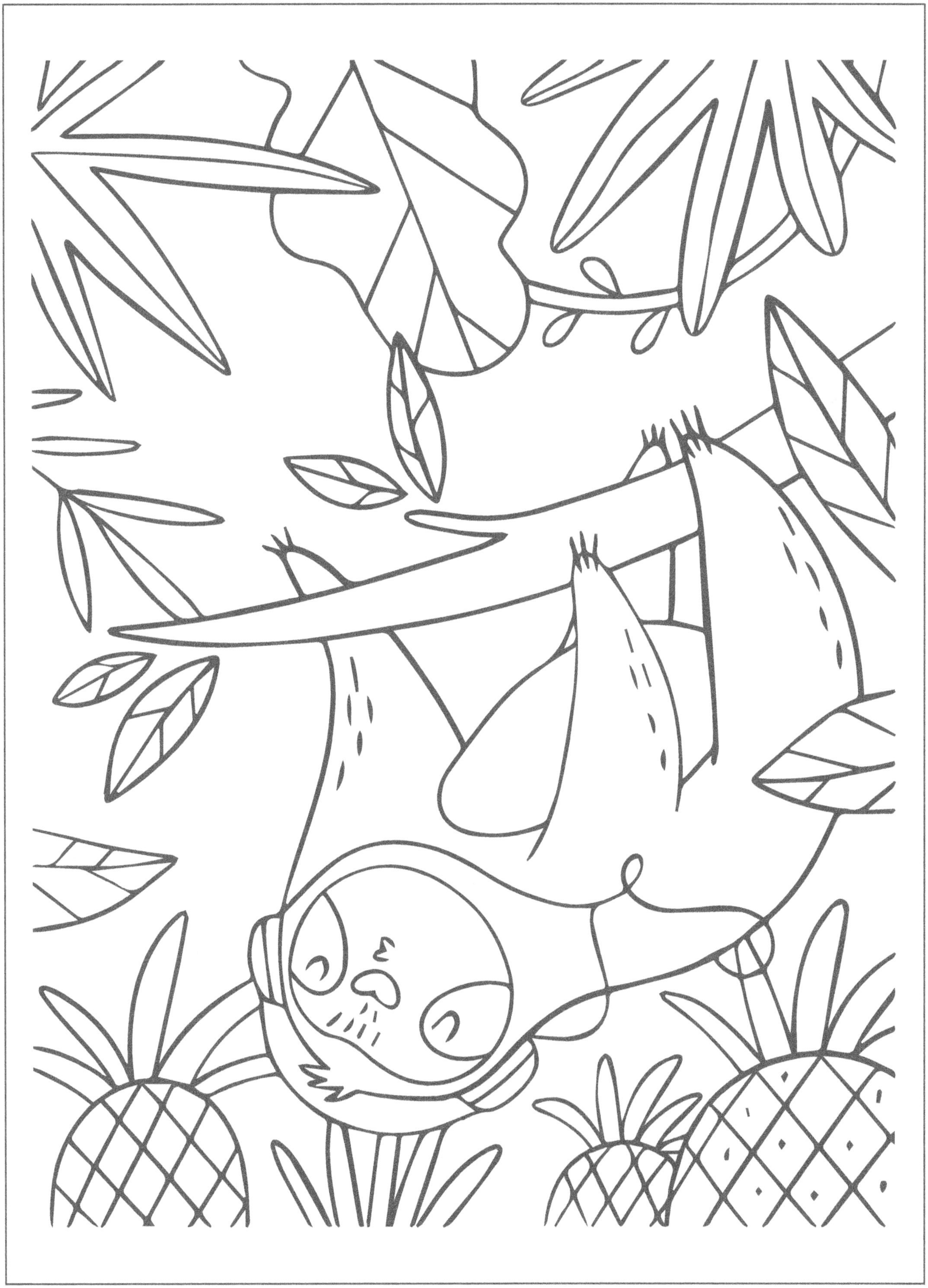

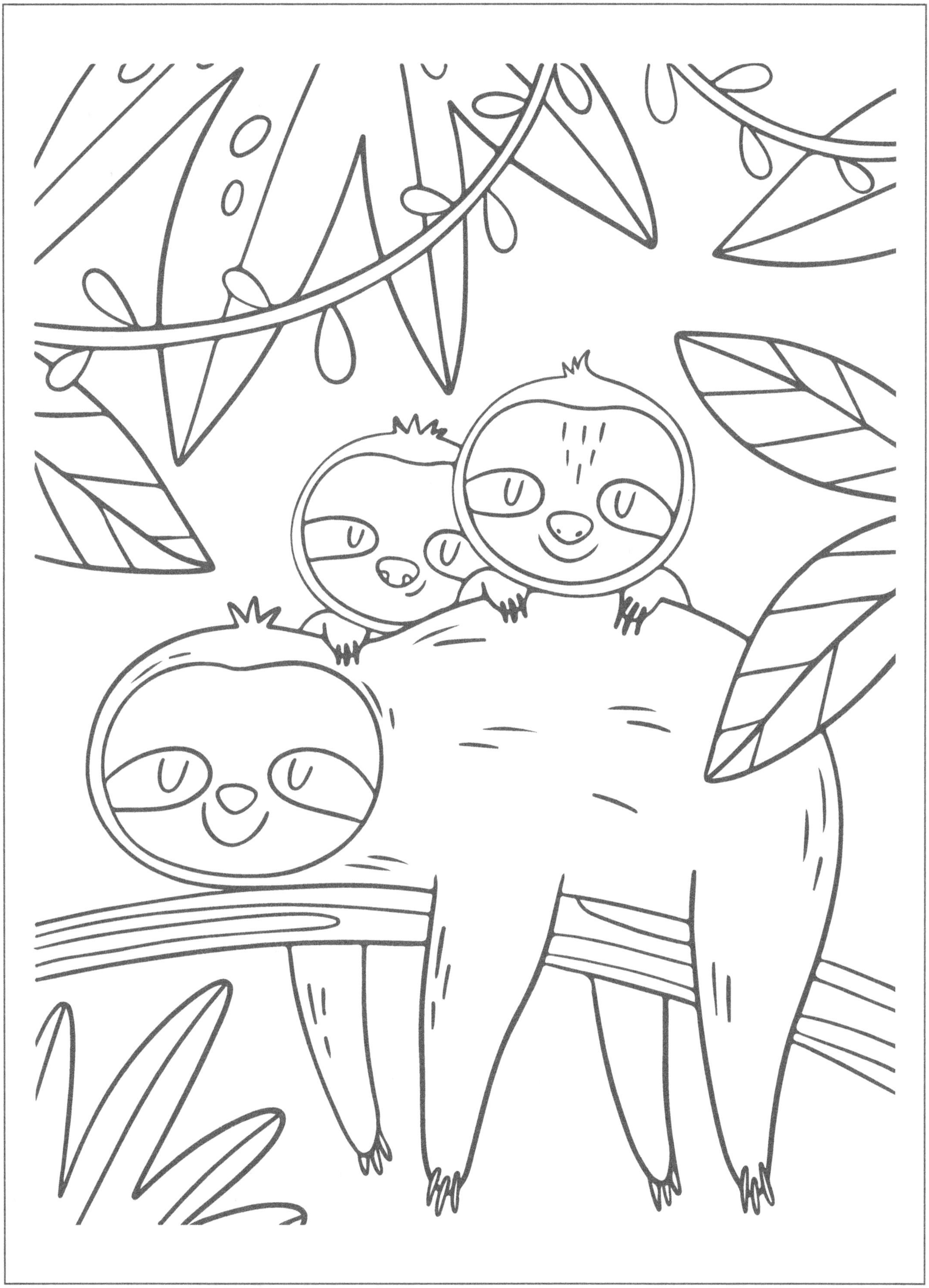

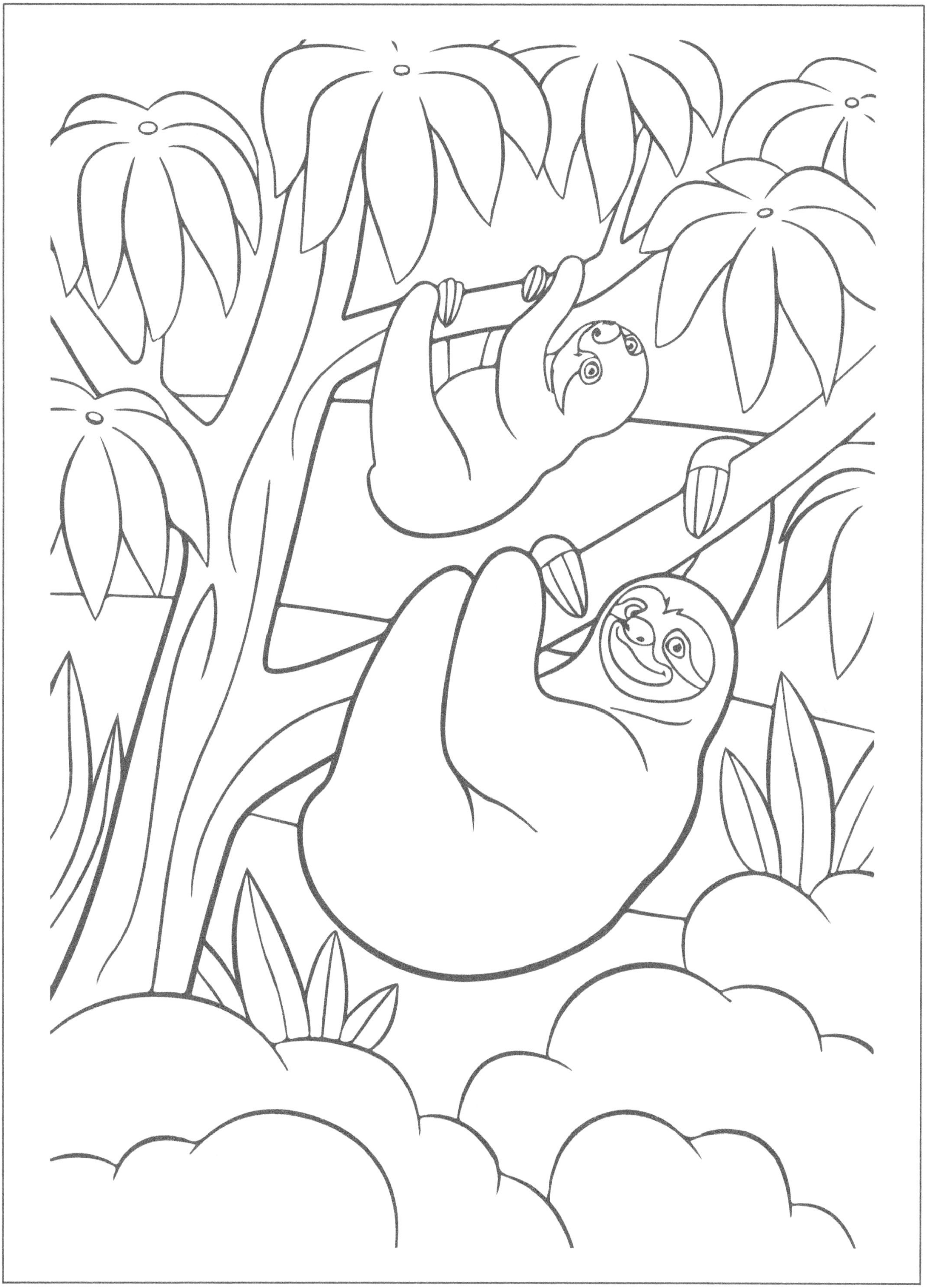

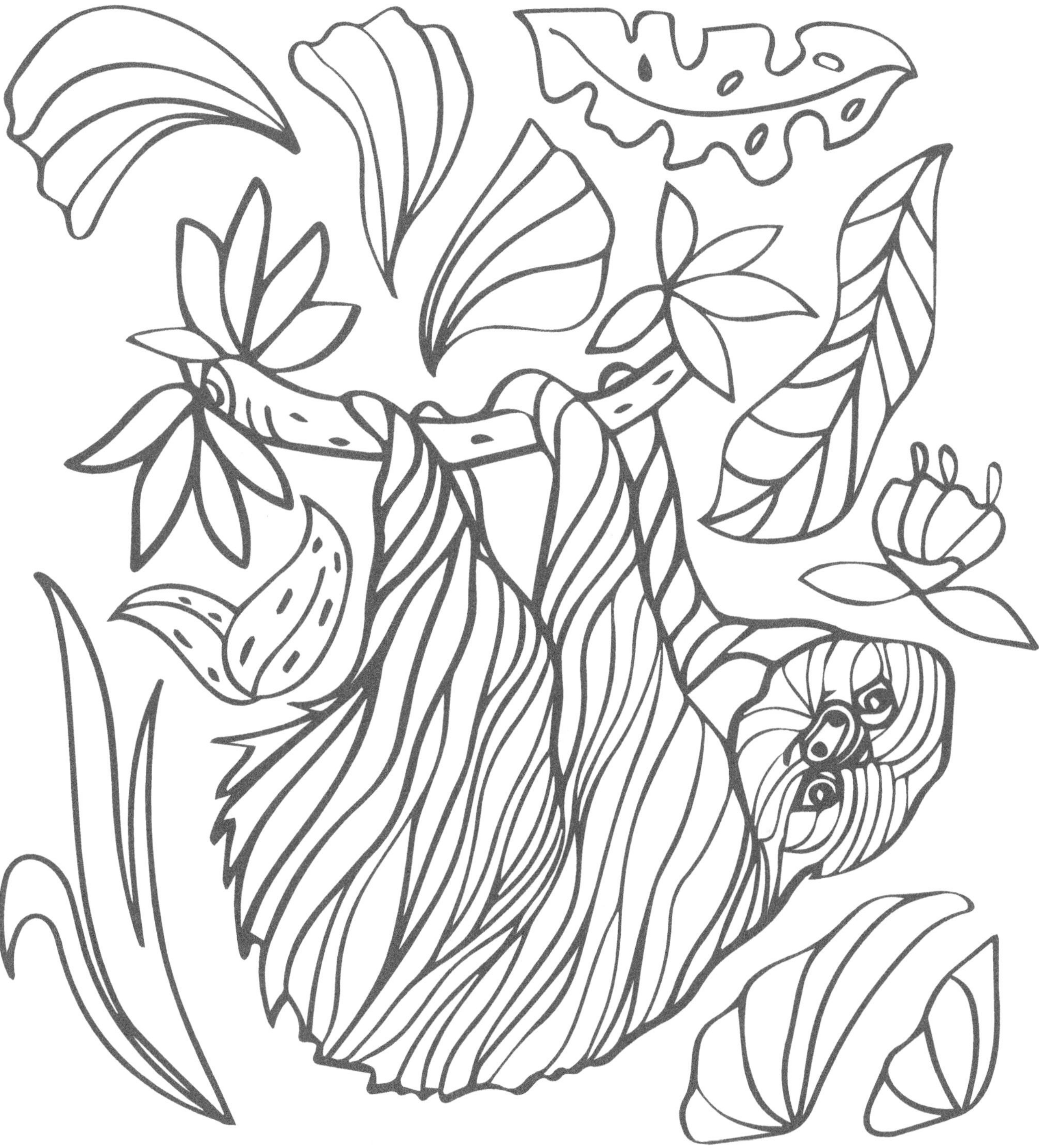

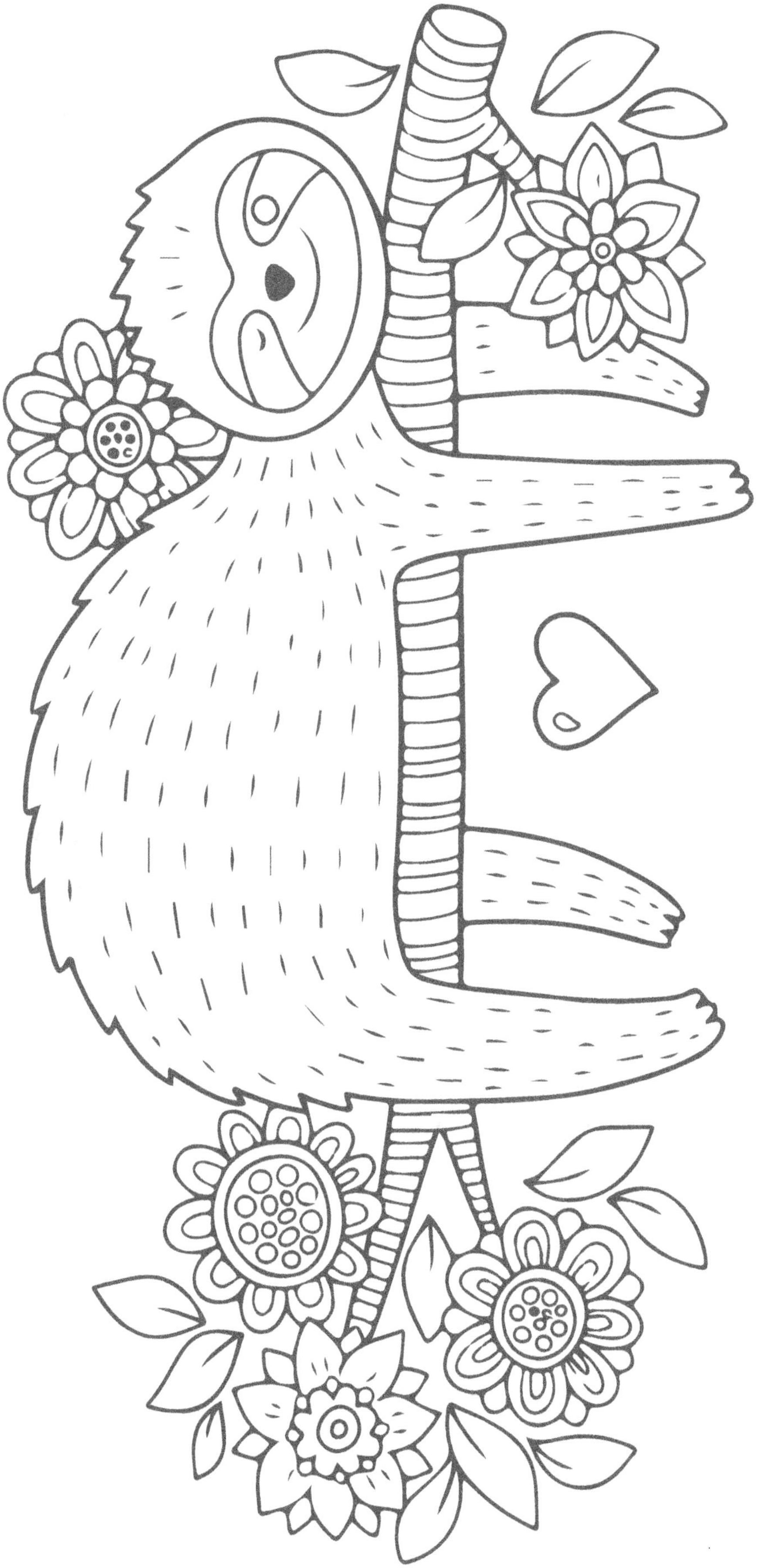

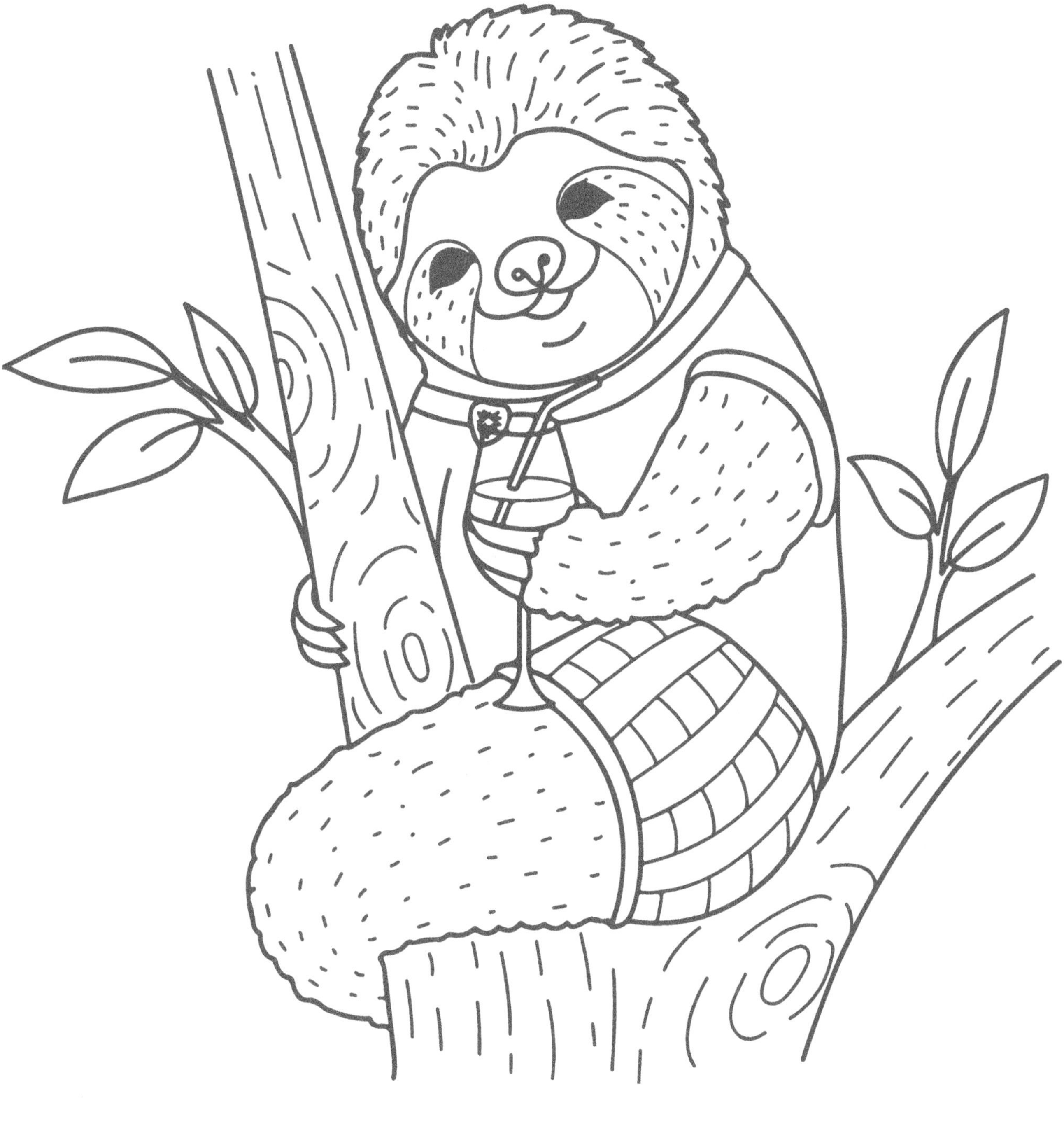

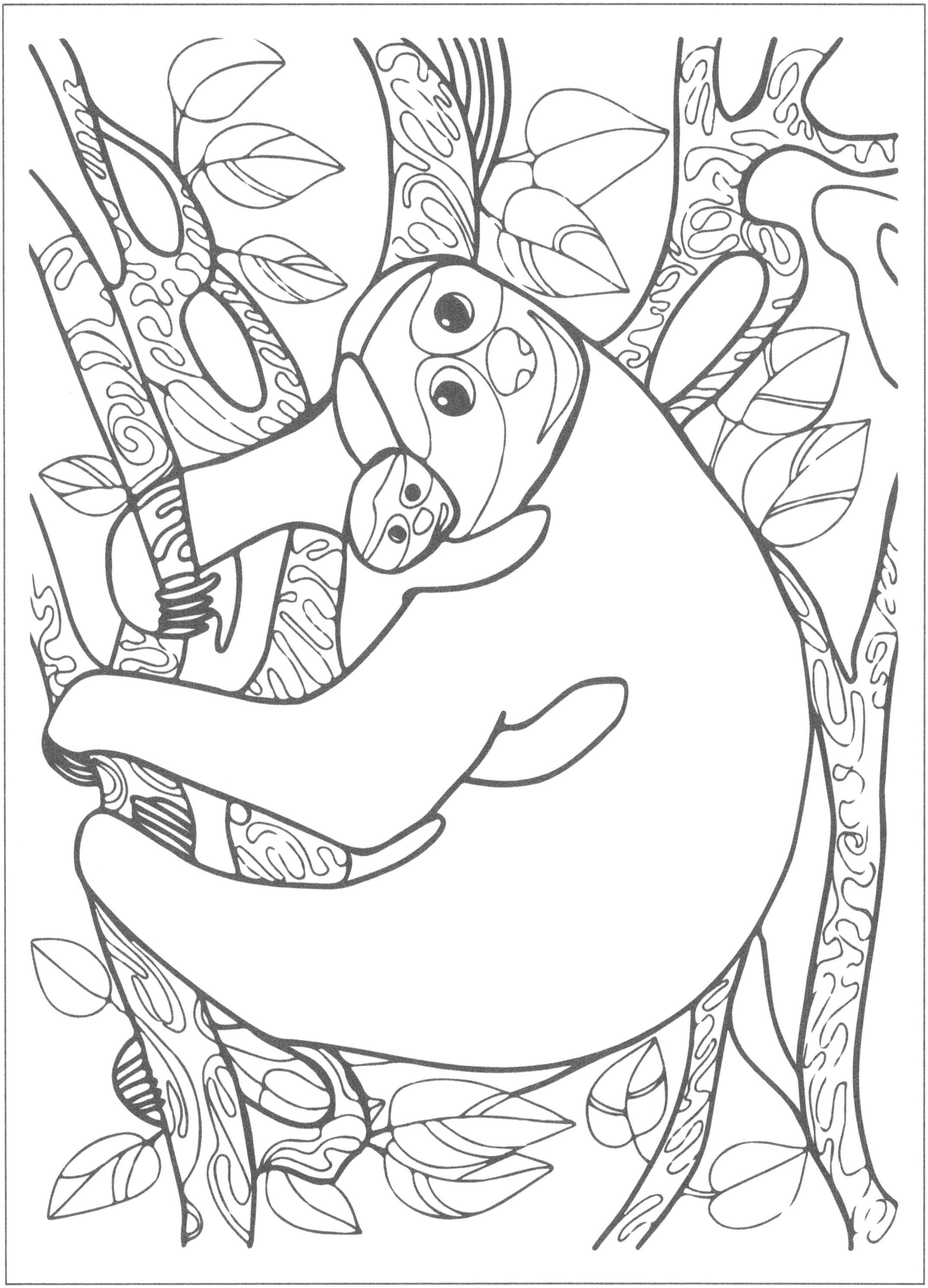

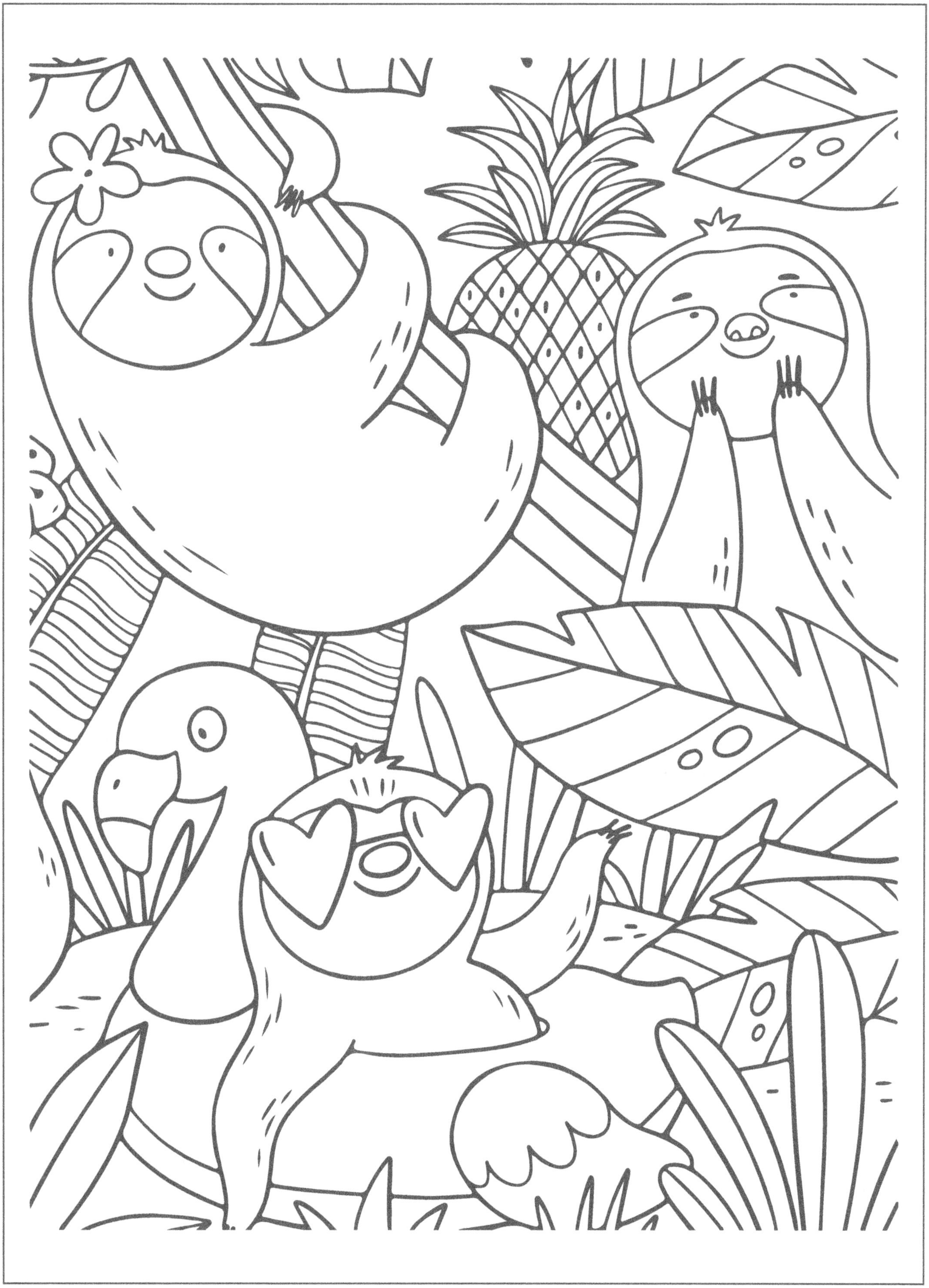

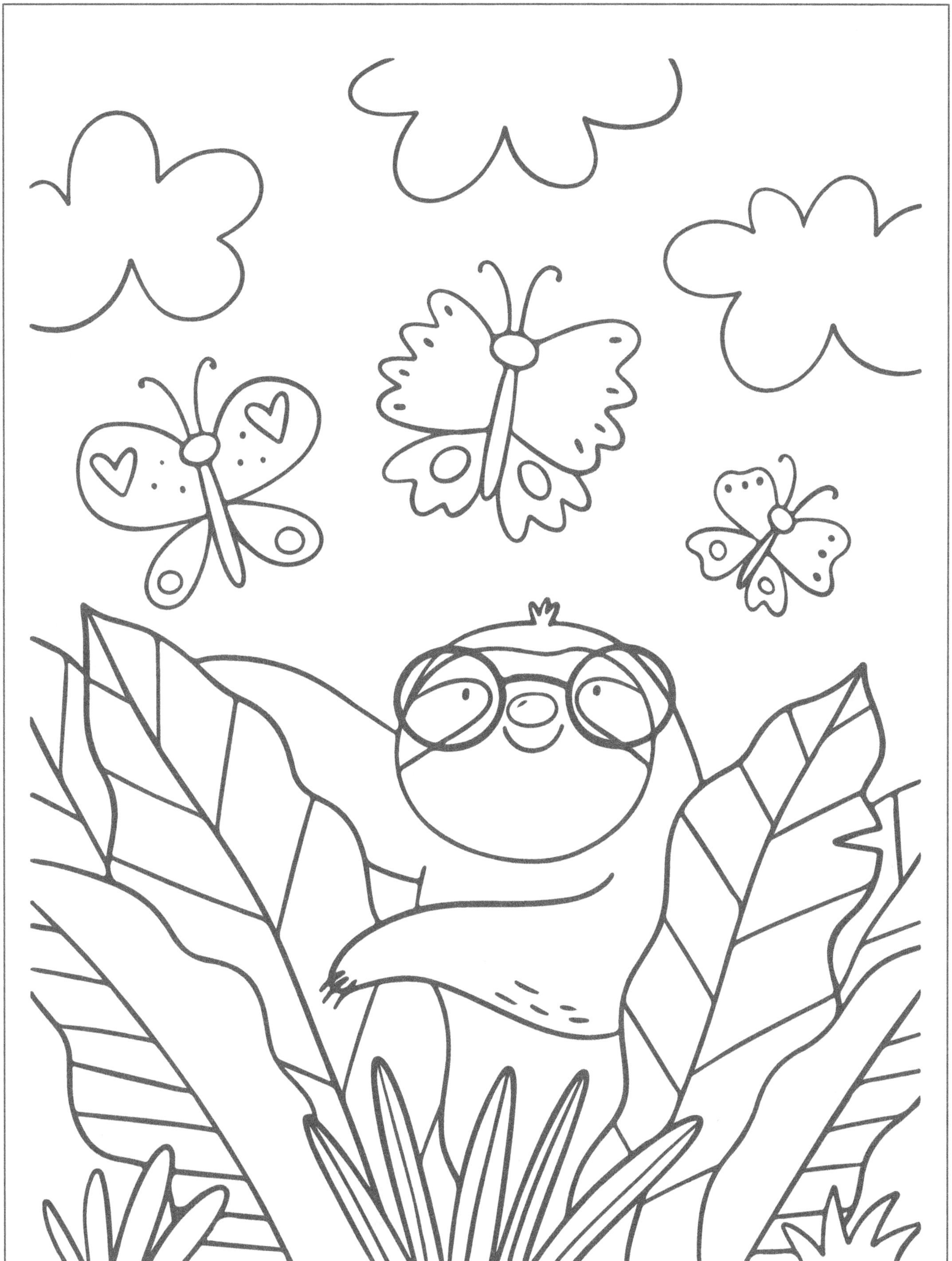

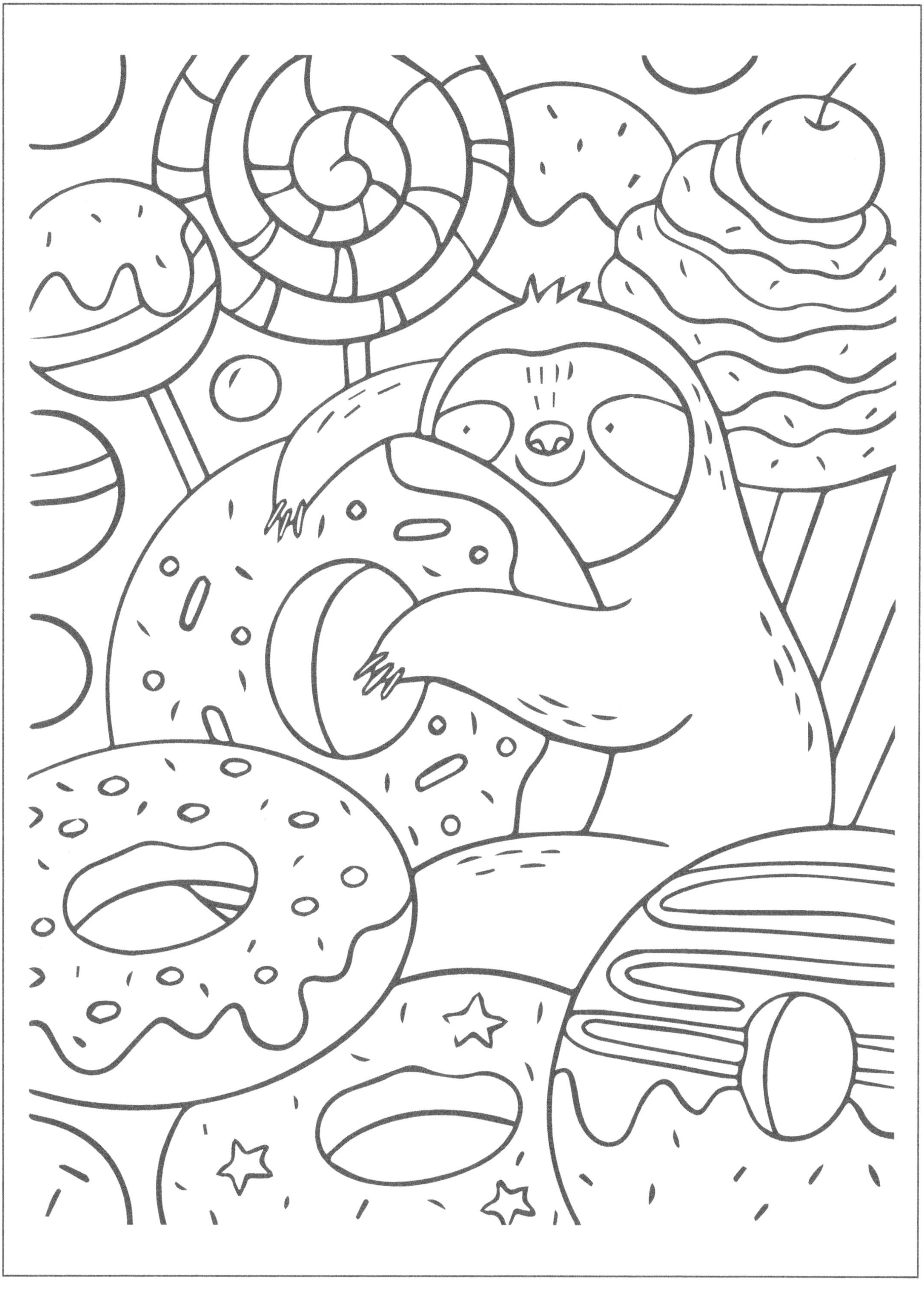

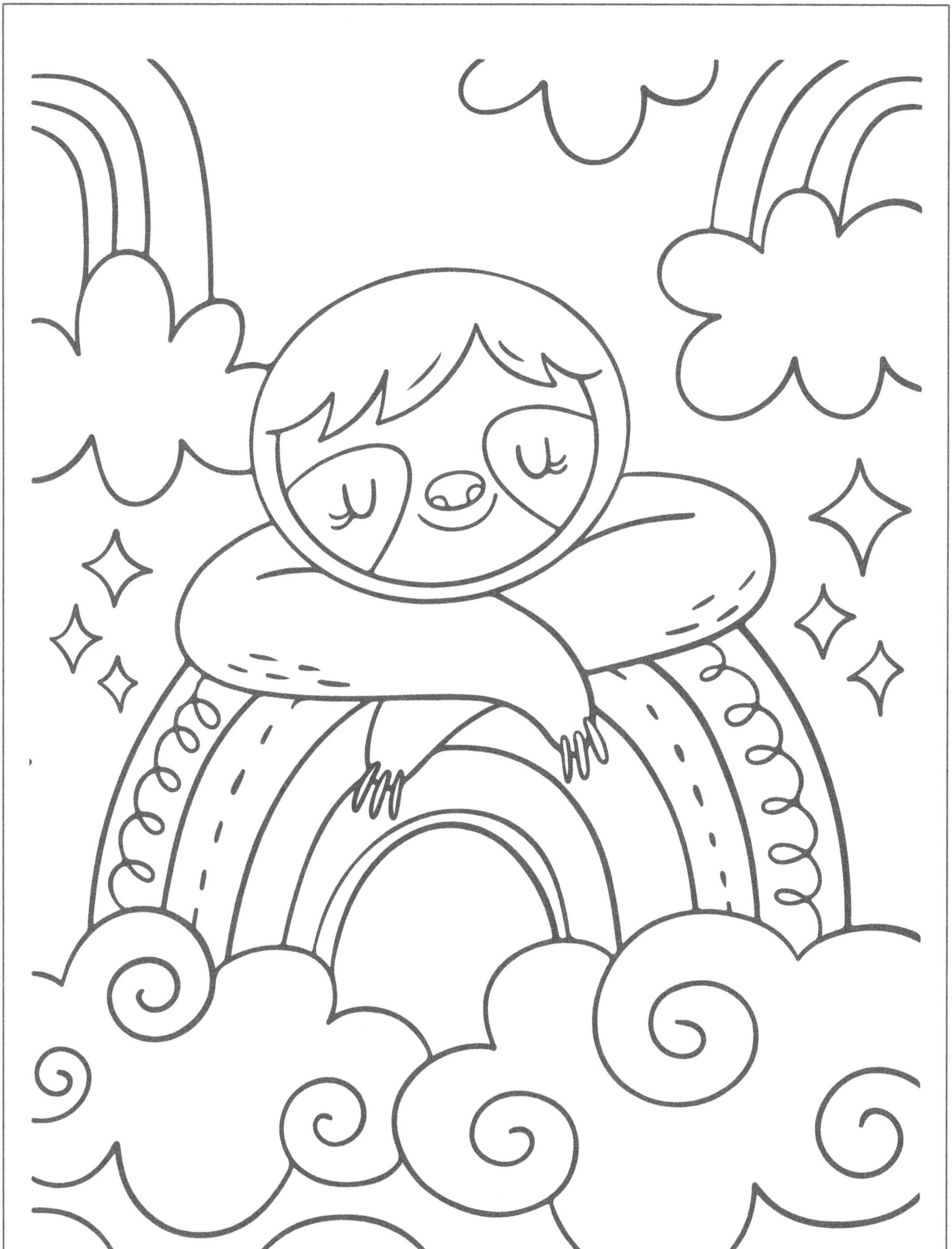

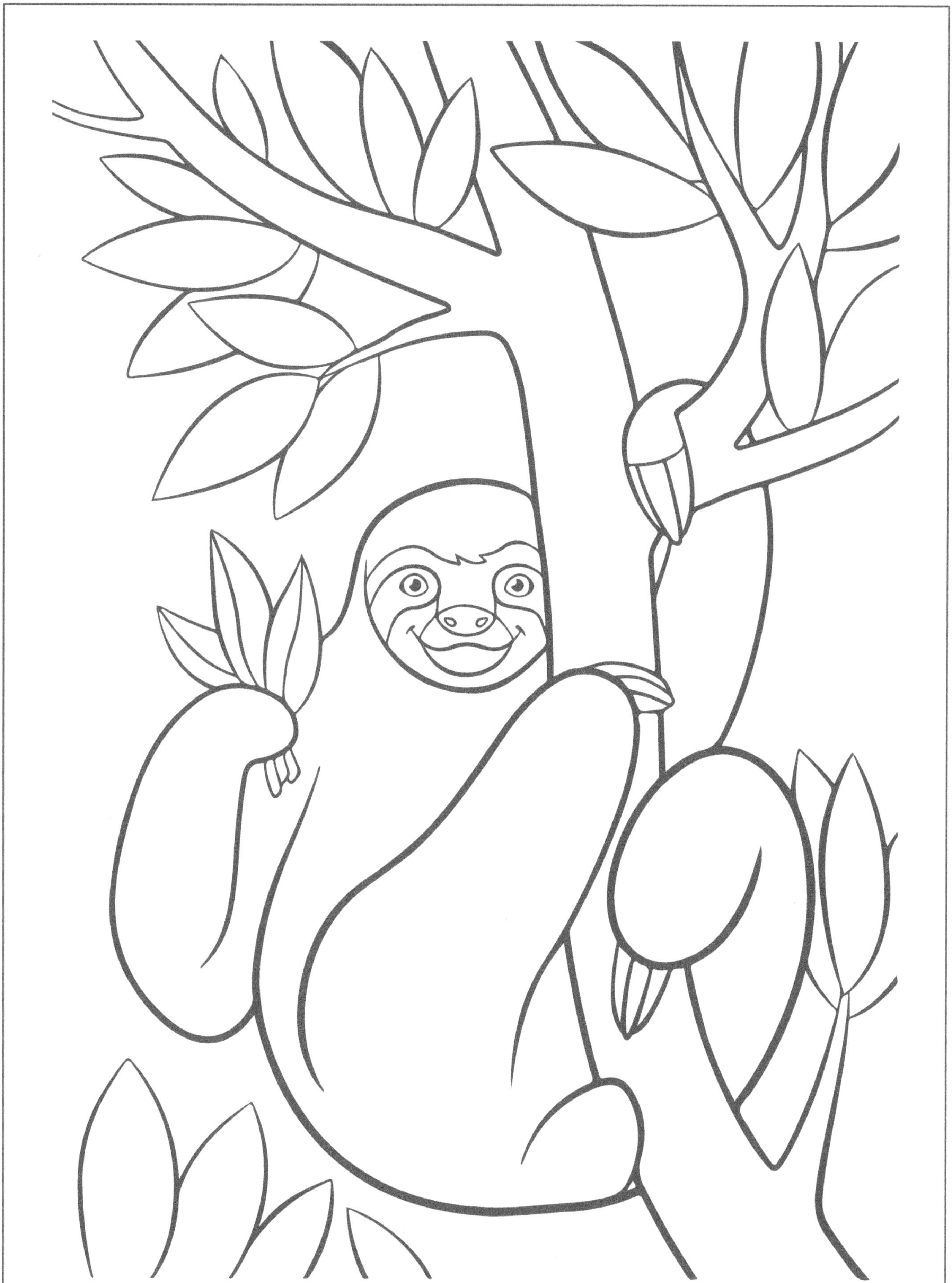

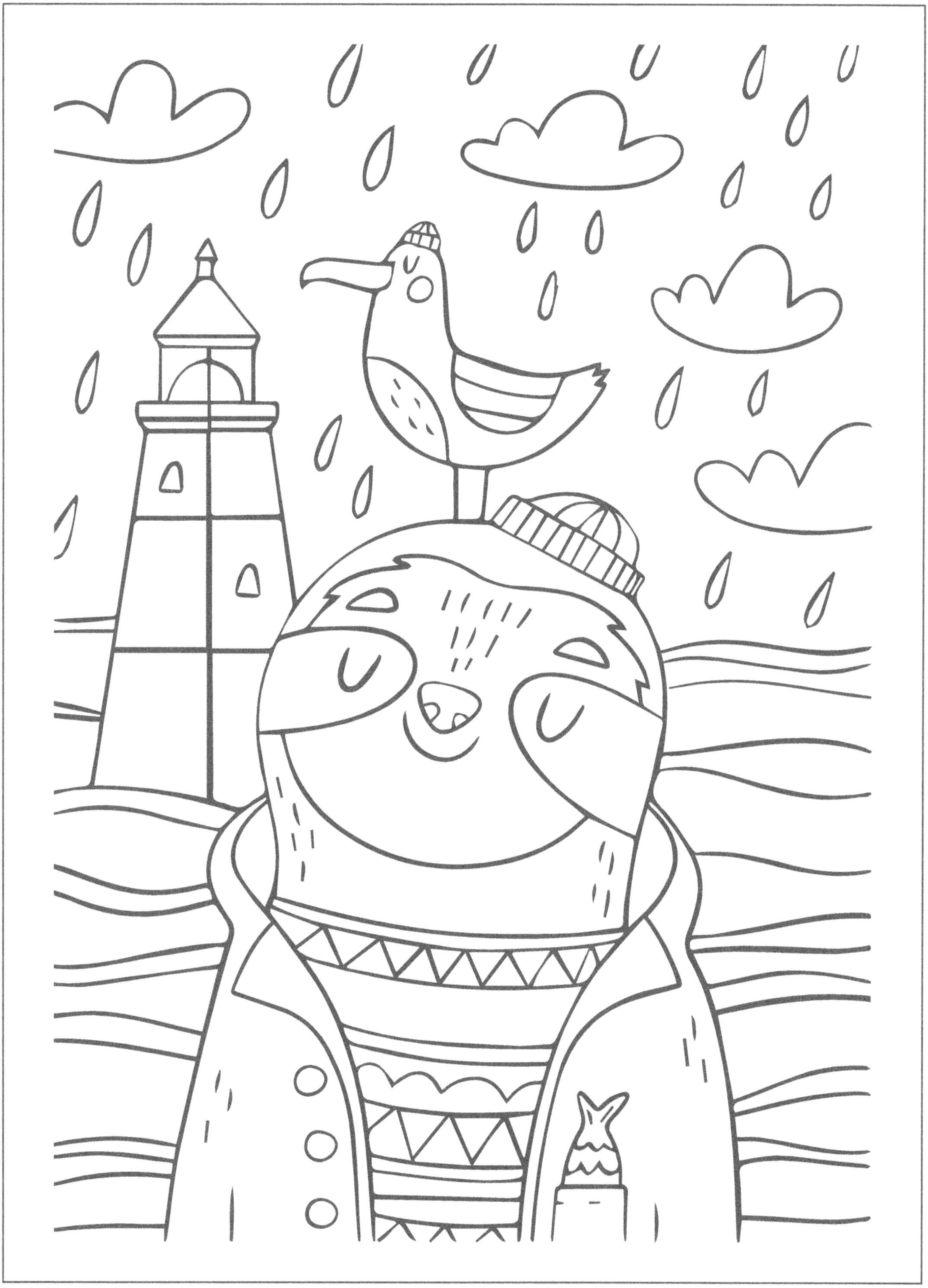

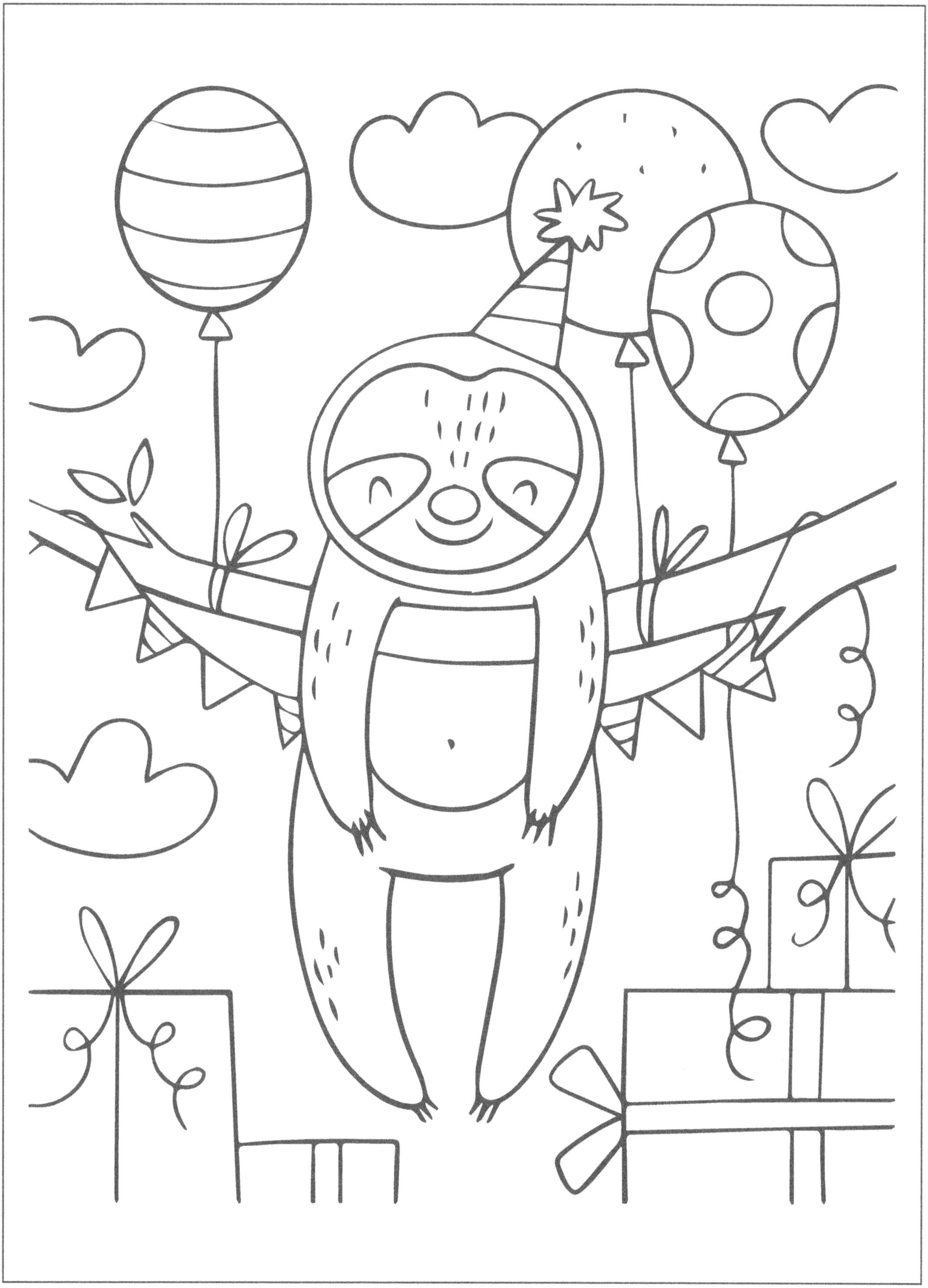

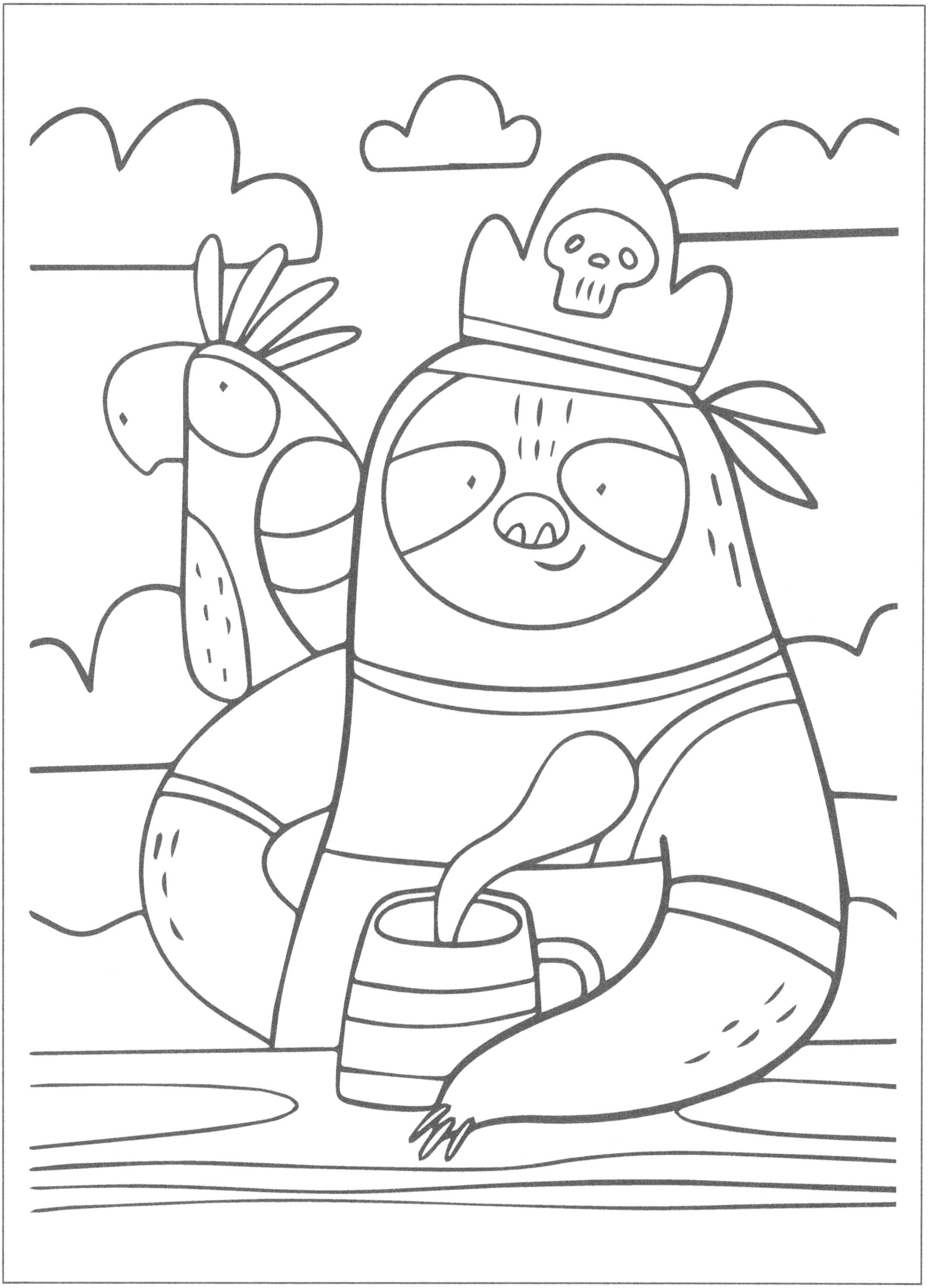

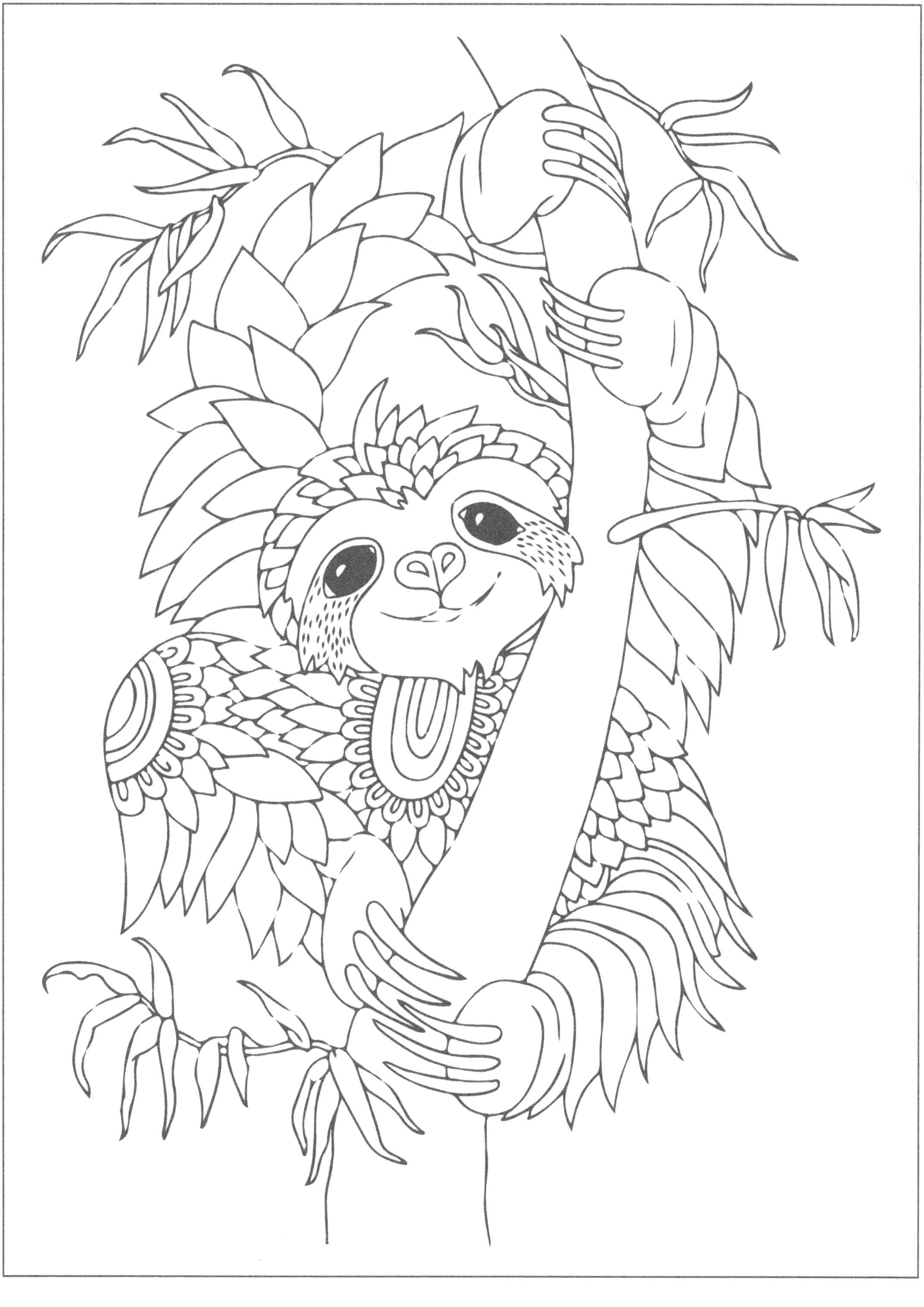

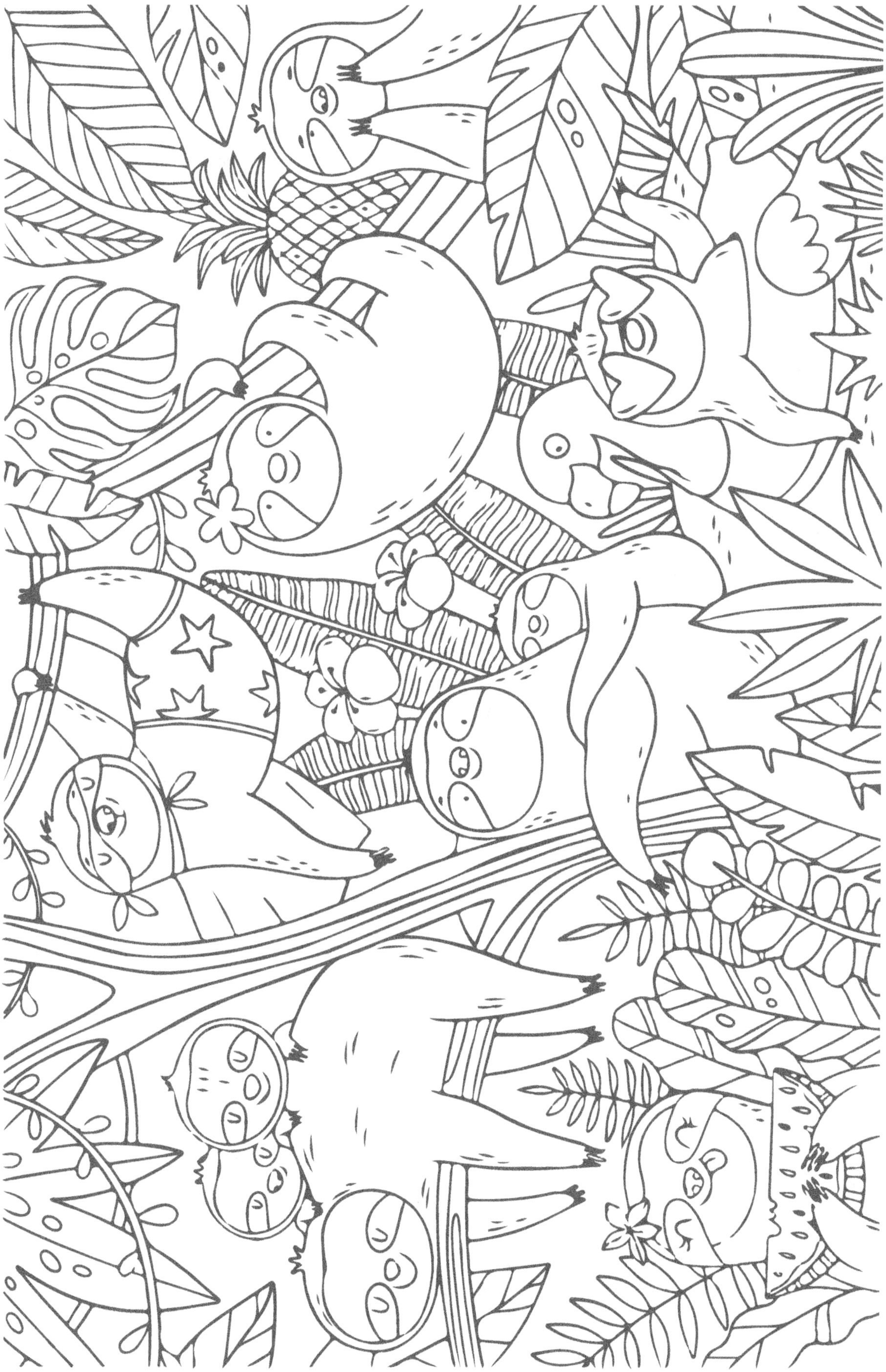

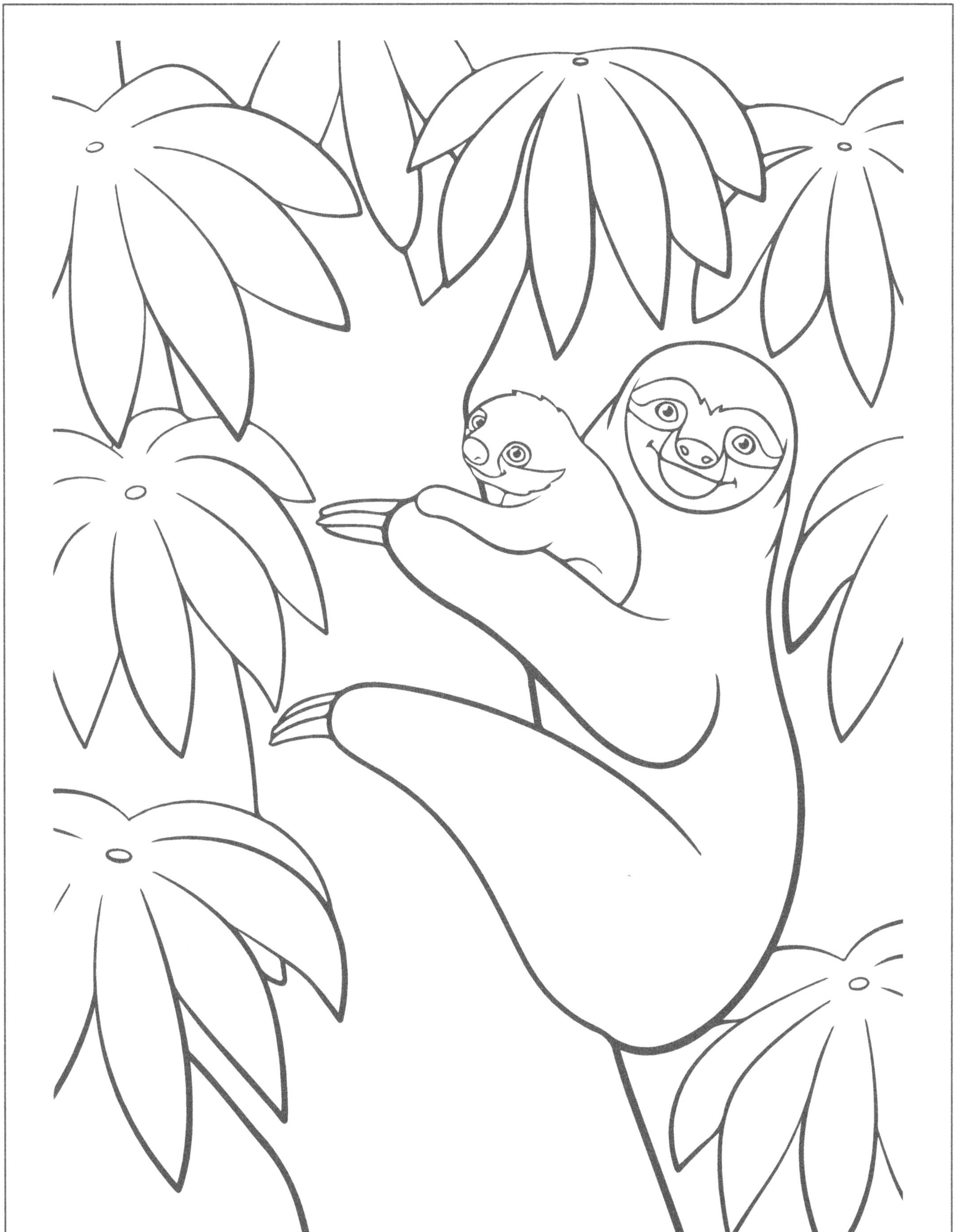

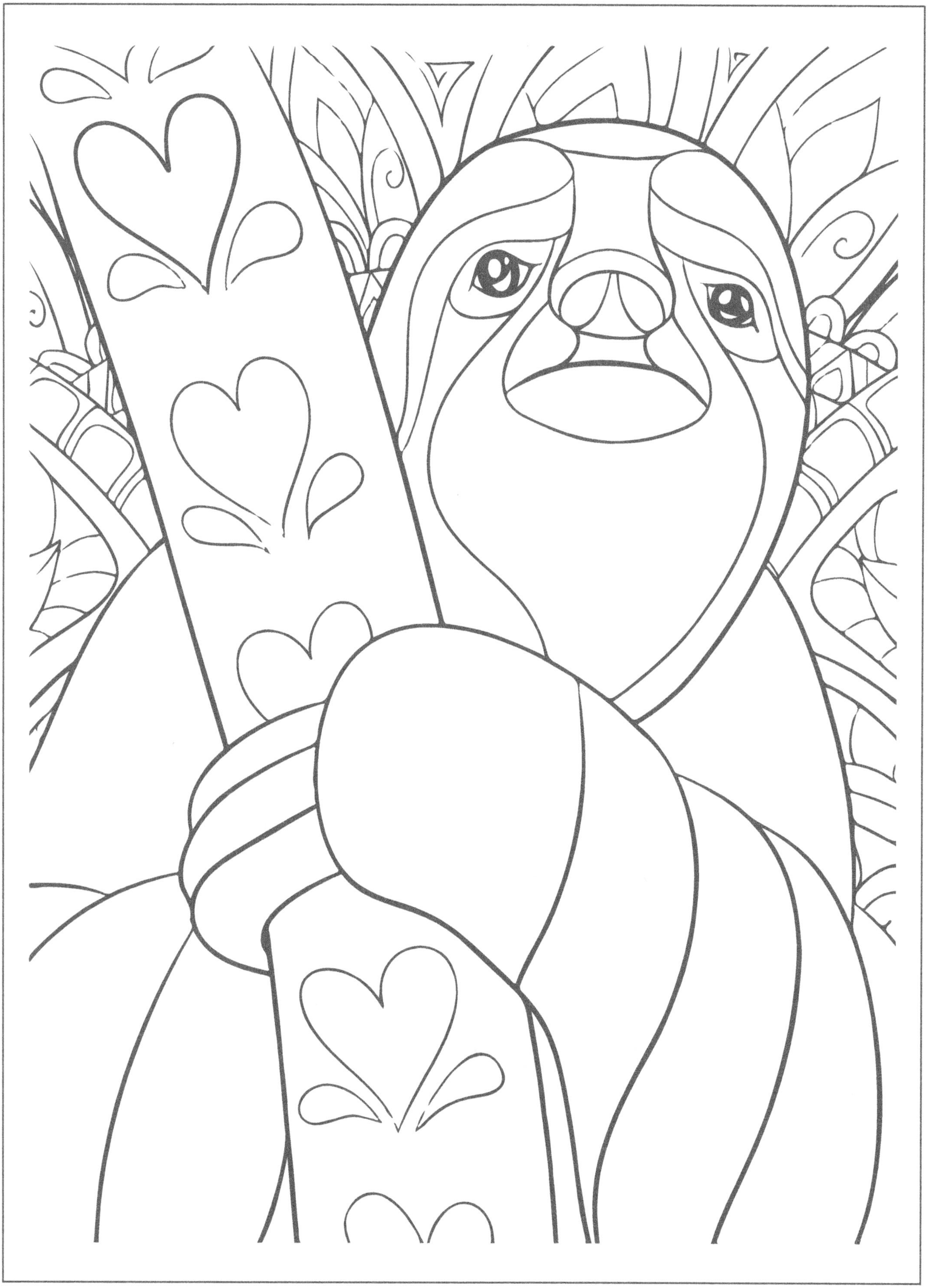

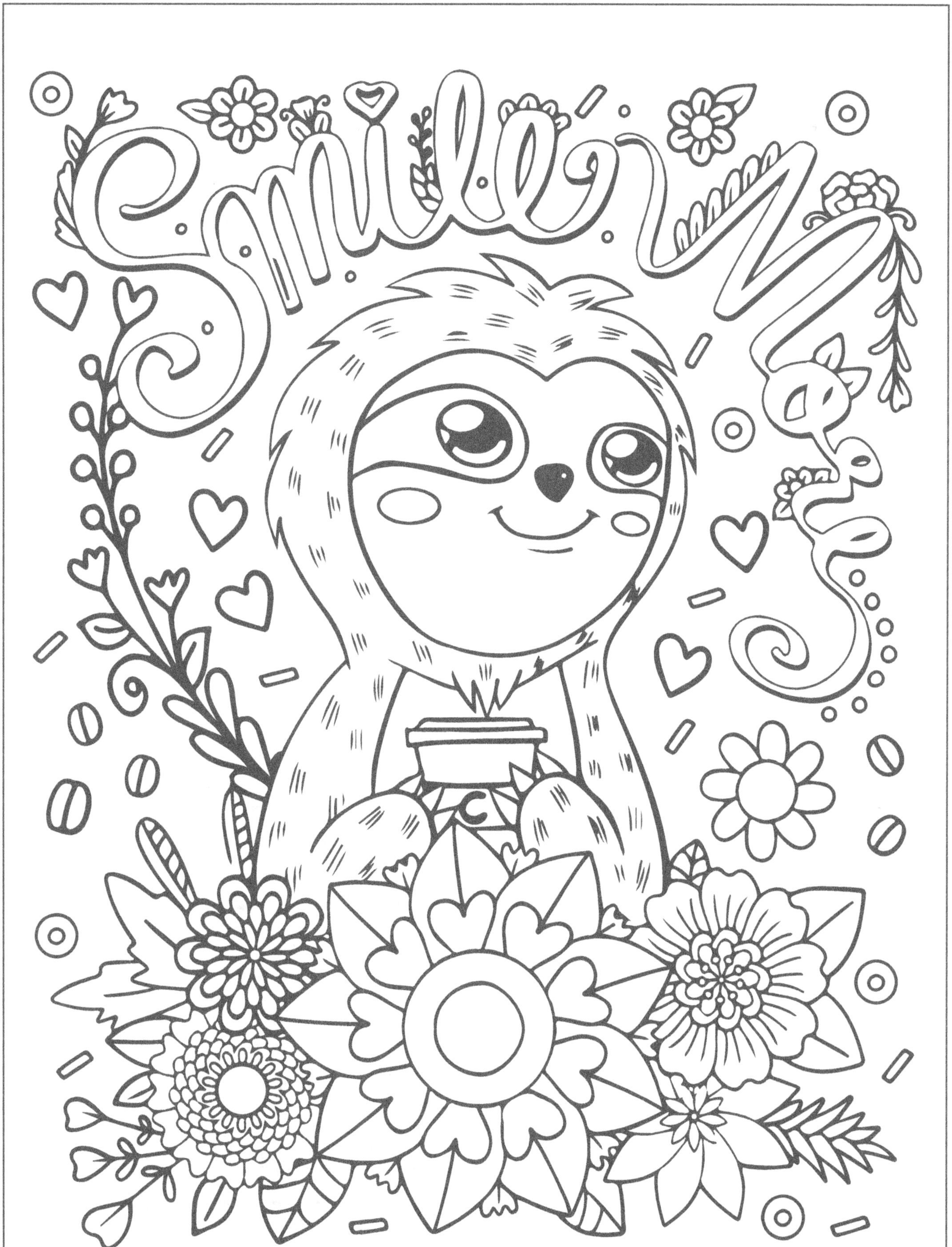
Smile More

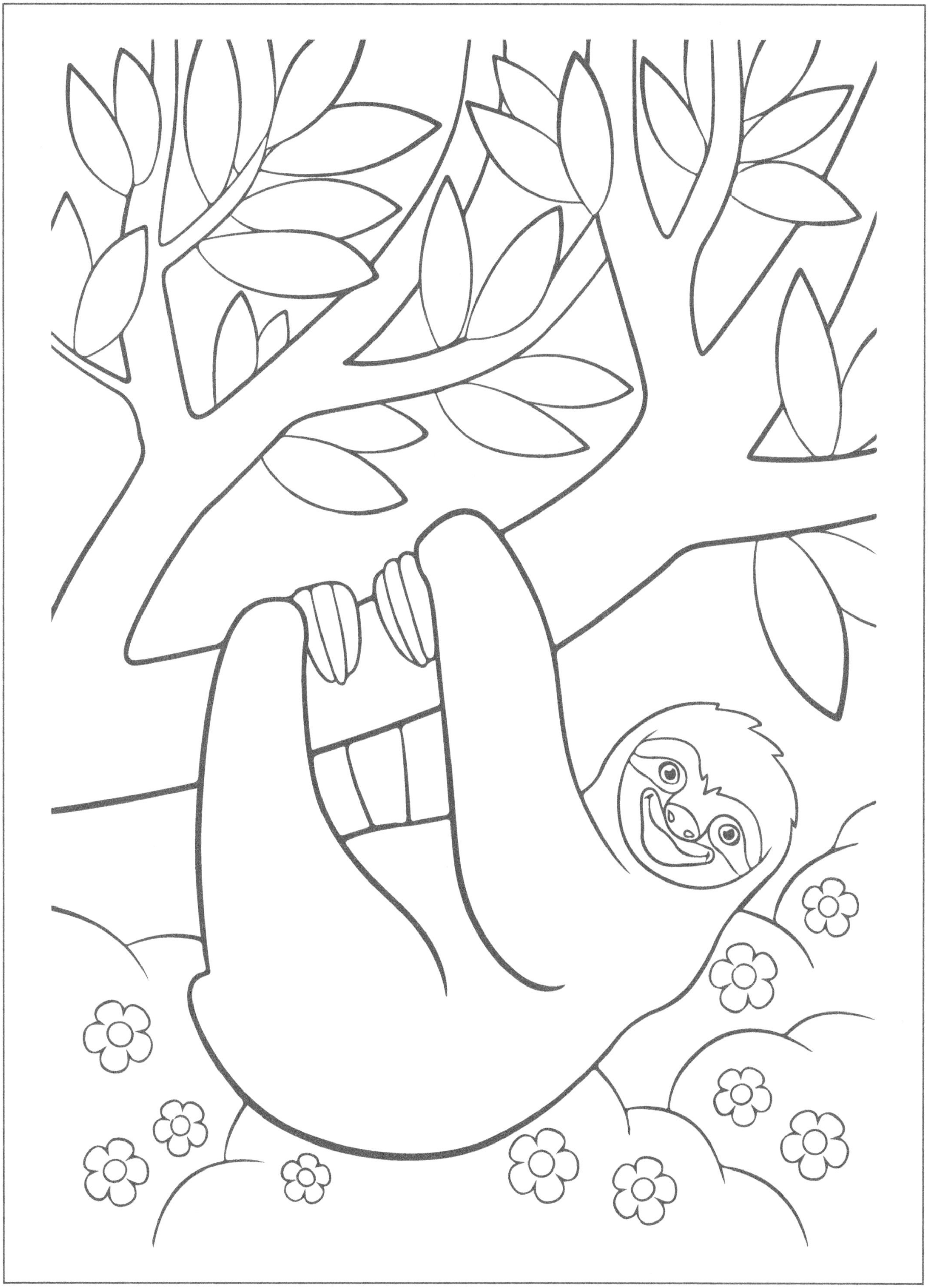

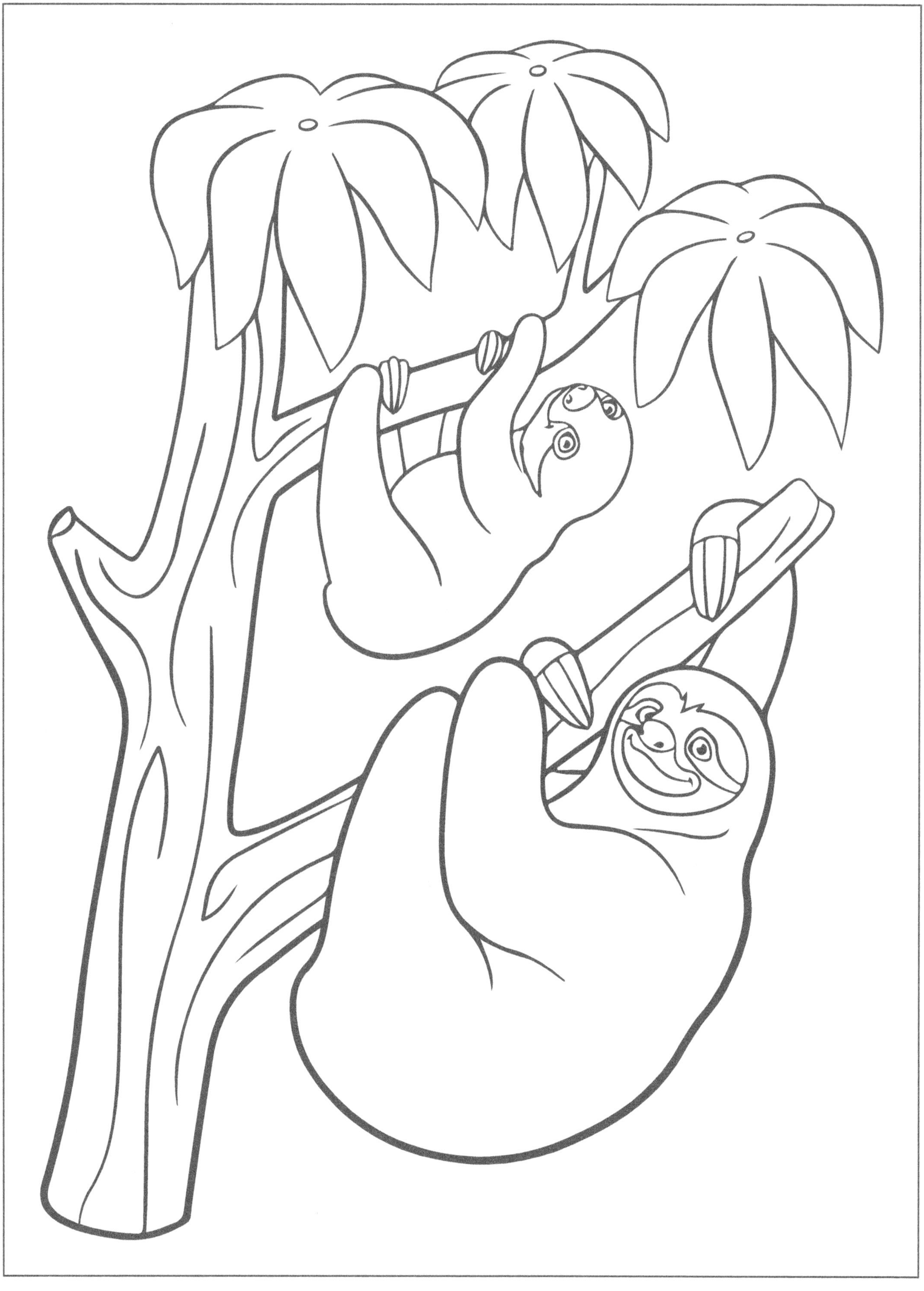

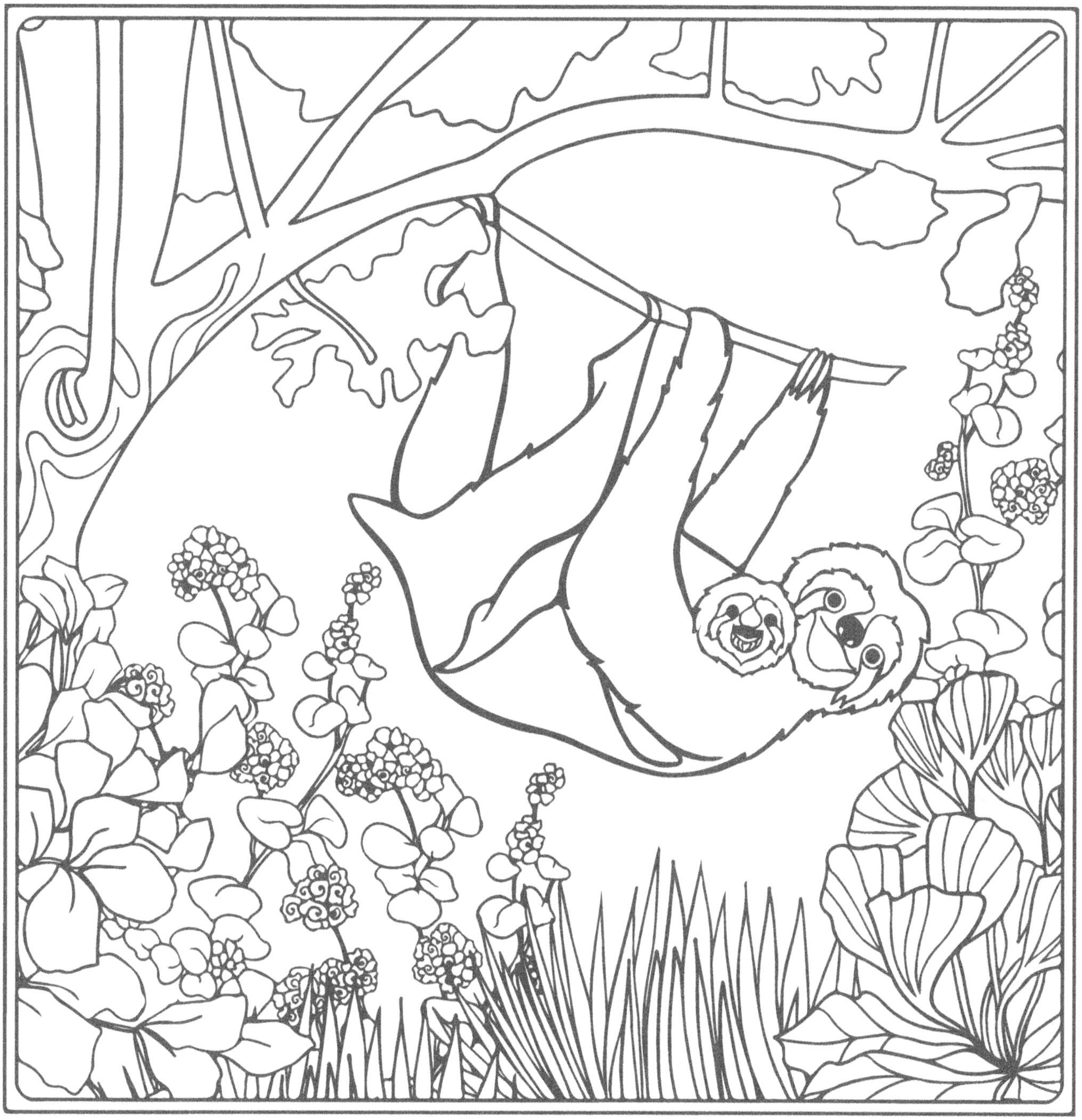

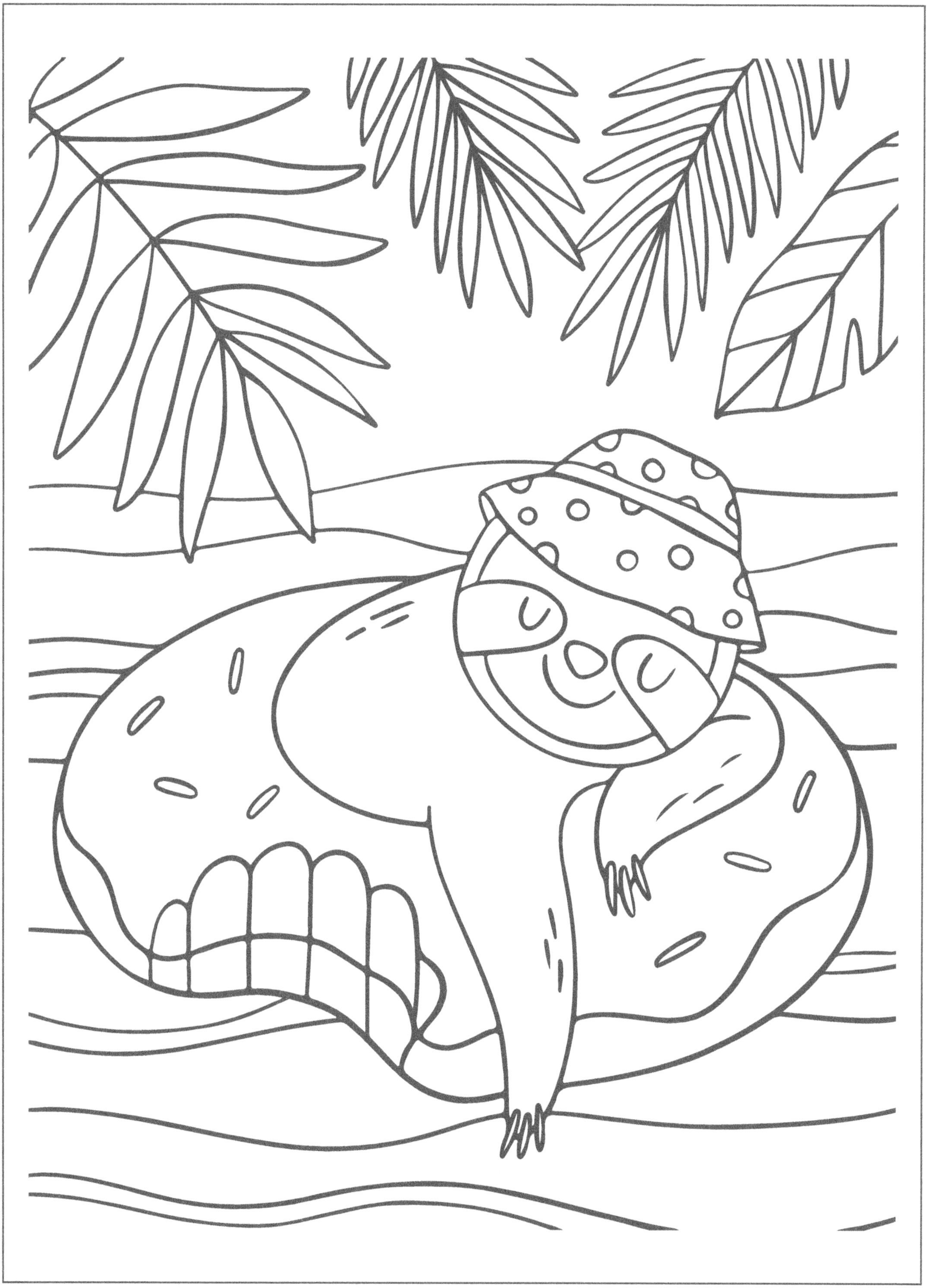

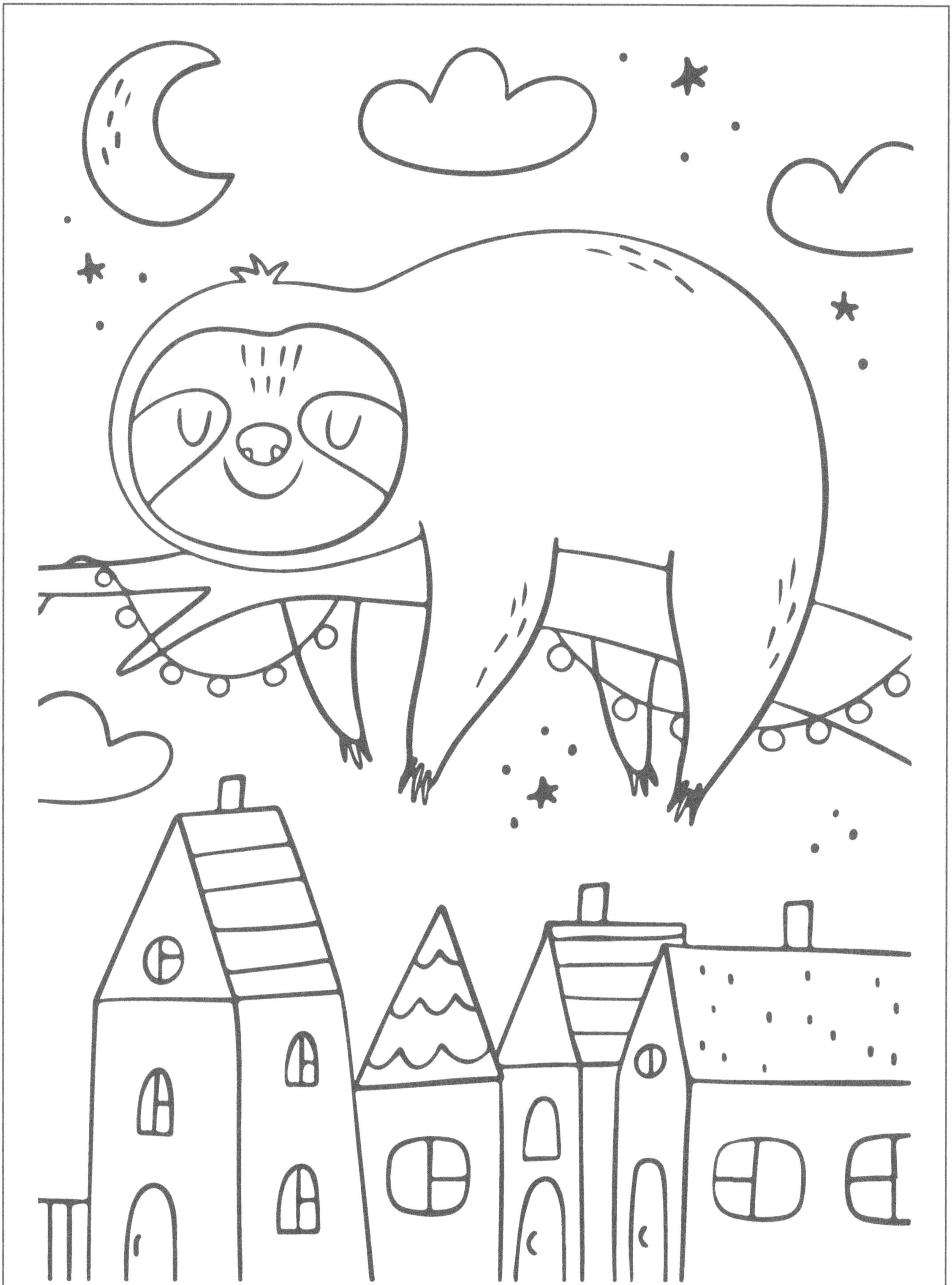

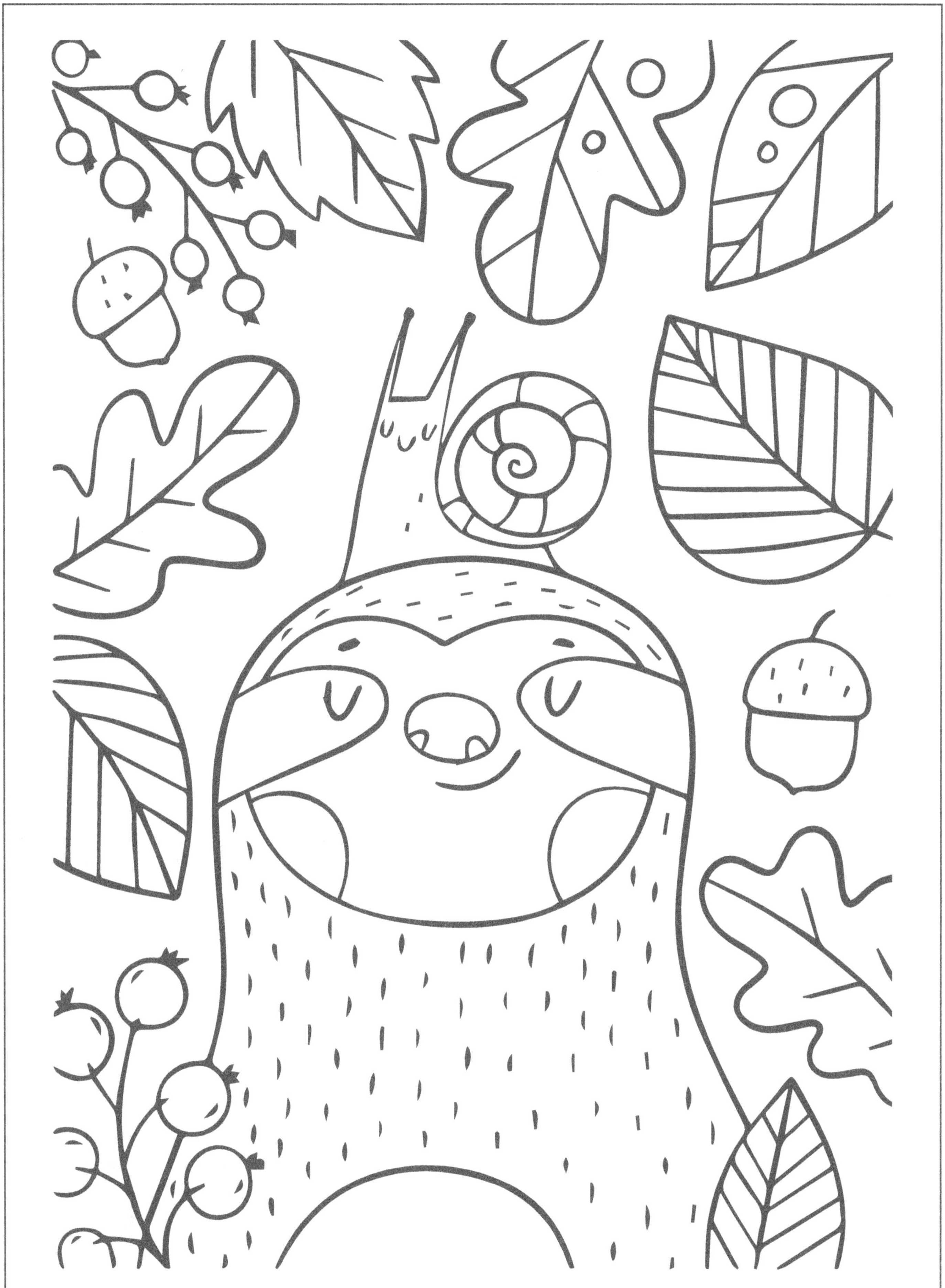

www.ingramcontent.com/pod-product-compliance
Lightning Source LLC
Chambersburg PA
CBHW081457220526
45466CB00008B/2689
* 9 7 9 8 5 8 6 2 2 2 6 3 3 *